Ed Cole

WITH NANCY CORBETT COLE

UNIQUE WOMAN

UNDERSTANDING HER GOD-GIVEN QUALITIES

WHITAKER
HOUSE

UNIQUE WOMAN:
Understanding Her God-Given Qualities

Christian Men's Network
P.O. Box 3
Grapevine, TX 76099
www.ChristianMensNetwork.com

Facebook.com/EdwinLouisCole

ISBN: 979-8-88769-144-2
Printed in the United States of America
© 2014 Edwin and Nancy Cole Legacy LLC

Whitaker House
1030 Hunt Valley Circle
New Kensington, PA 15068
www.whitakerhouse.com

1 2 3 4 5 6 7 8 9 10 11 **LJ** 31 30 29 28 27 26 25 24

DEDICATION

TO OUR MOTHERS

To the courageous women who helped
shape our lives—

Florence Goodrum Cole
Alice Miriam Corbett

CONTENTS

FOREWORD

You are unique! There are no two people who are just alike. God created each of us uniquely different. He has given each of us unique personalities and giftings that He desires for us to use to bring Him glory.

My prayer is that whether you are a man or woman, old or young, you receive the wisdom provided in *Unique Woman*. This book could be instrumental in saving your marriage or changing your life. I believe that as you read it, you will grow to a new level in your walk with God that will be recognized by others.

When we come into relationship with Jesus Christ, and begin to seek Him, He begins to unfold His plan for our lives. He gives us His grace to do whatever we are called to do. Because we live in a fallen world, there are tests, temptations, and trials that come in various forms to our lives. It is only through learning God's voice—His thoughts and His ways—that we are able to rise above circumstances and fulfill His plan.

Through the years, I have known women from various backgrounds and ages that have stood out among the crowd in being all God wanted them to be. This was because they had come to know the Lord in a day-by-day experience, being secure in who they were in Him, seeking His wisdom for their lives, and seeking to make a difference in the lives of others whom God placed them with.

Proverbs tells us that wisdom from God is the main thing we need in life. It requires knowing His voice and obeying Him. Proverbs 14:1 says, *"The wise woman builds her house, but the foolish* [woman] *tears it down with her hands."* God's Word reveals His wisdom to us. The wise woman learns how to allow God's grace to guide her in whatever circumstance in which she finds herself.

Two people who have been instrumental in showing people how to take God's principles of wisdom and walk it out have been Ed and Nancy Cole. Dr. Cole for many years focused on helping Christian men become leaders and promise keepers. He and his wife Nancy felt led to put their years of wise counsel into a book that could help women rise to fulfill God's plan in life.

In this book, Ed and Nancy speak to both single and married women. They bring out the balanced teaching of the marriage relationship and address topics such as submission, forgiveness, sex, stay-at-home moms, moms working outside of the home, seasons of life, myths about males and females, and how to be the fulfilled woman God planned for you to be. There is so much in this book that I believe you will refer back to, even after you have read it.

My late husband Billy Joe and I were blessed to have known Ed and Nancy personally. Their teachings and their lives were consistent and they have impacted many lives through the years. Ed and Nancy are a father and mother in the Christian faith.

The following pages contain more than mere words of man because they hold real truths that can be lived out in real life.

~ Sharon Daugherty
Senior Pastor, Victory Christian Center
Tulsa, Oklahoma

PREFACE

At the outset of this book, let me tell you about the author, Nancy, my wife of more than fifty years before she left me for another Man—the Man Christ Jesus.

Nancy was the embodiment of the word "grace." Known around the world as "The Loveliest Lady in the Land," she was loved by those who knew her, and she loved those she knew. She was courageous, firm, loving, gentle, beautiful and the most godly person I ever knew in my lifetime.

The following pages contain the pattern of what made her "unique" and are the only place where she revealed in words her beliefs about true femininity and womanhood, at every stage of a woman's life.

Through the years of our marriage, I grew to love her in a way I never dreamed was possible. Her prayer life, forgiving spirit, consistent application of truth, never-ending compassion and humor were a constant source of strength to me and to her entire family.

These pages contain a priceless legacy from a life lived in intimate friendship with God and man, giving you the principles, truths, insights and revelations that guided, sustained and kept her. They were learned at a great price, but shared with you freely. Learn them to avoid the cost of the lessons.

Throughout my life, I have had the opportunity to meet, study under, work with and befriend some of the world's finest people. For each and every one who has profoundly influenced my life, I thank God. However, without any doubt, my wife was the single greatest influence on my life.

Nancy's life was lived with a passion to introduce people to Jesus Christ. Through her writings, you may come to know and love her and learn to love the Lord of her life more than ever. She would want it that way.

~ Edwin Louis Cole

ACKNOWLEDGMENT

To our daughter, Joann Webster,
for her hard work, for the hours she expended
writing, researching—painstakingly
pulling the manuscript together. We couldn't
have done it without her.

INTRODUCTION

Since World War II, society's image of woman has shifted as quickly as the fashion trends. The ideal touted in one season becomes outmoded the next. One season women's groups and the world's media are promoting a "feminist movement," then a few years later, the movement is being called an "unfortunate, embarrassing relic of the Sixties."

One year "Supermom" is lauded, and the next she is abased. A New York management consultant says, "Marketers are (now) treating women as if they were—I don't know how else to say it—as if they were regular people."[1]

Each image and ideal, portrayed as the new, improved version (like packaged products), somehow is beyond the grasp of "regular people." And each successive "ideal" proves to be as confining and constricting to women as those of the past.

Many women embark on a search for the "real me" only to be deceived or frustrated as they attempt to become whatever is the present-day image of woman. Outwardly conforming, yet inwardly rebelling, they one day discover that, deep inside, they are not the person they have accidentally become.

Others are afraid to admit what they really desire to become. They hesitate to talk about what they believe is their real potential. Repression seems easier to deal with than rejection.

Some women have learned to seek and receive roses, dinners and diamonds—yet they never have the stability, security, satisfaction of identity or real love they truly desire.

A great number of women have given their lives over to men, wanting to live through husbands and boyfriends—only to be disappointed in the men and, as a result, in themselves.

Many, many wives desperately want their husbands to change, mature, accept responsibility and be the men they were created to be. They realize belatedly that the only truly liberated married woman is married to a "maximized" man.

Single women want to find "Mr. Right." Most of them do not realize they will not find "right" men while looking in the "wrong" places.

Ours is a world of disposable diapers, disposable razors and disposable women. Women are deserted and discarded every day. Convenience outweighs commitment.

Disappointed and dissatisfied, women seek legislation to cause society to change. They verbally demand for people to change. And, inwardly, they long for their personal lives to change.

What is the standard of measure to determine the changes that need to be made?

Who are the people who must do the changing?

And who will enforce the changes?

Where is there justice and power?

There is only one true standard, one great authority, one perfect justice, one source of power that is able to withstand and outlast the tests of time, pressures of society, ever-changing authorities and fluctuations in the world. That authority and power is found in Jesus Christ—Savior of all, Lord of Life—and in His eternal truth.

True womanhood can never be measured by a man's affections or society's praises but by a woman's own character as measured by the Word of God.

There is no other standard.

We attempt, in these next pages, to pass on to you some of God's truths, principles and patterns to help you attain a higher goal, achieve a better life and enjoy richer relationships.

This is not an exhaustive commentary on womanhood. Nor is it a concordance of advice, one of the thousands of "self-help" books or a formula for success. This book simply contains some of the truths we have learned from our life together during many years of marriage and ministry.

So, relax and read.

Then apply and enjoy.

Truth is like soap—it won't do you any good if it is not applied.

~ Edwin and Nancy Cole

CHAPTER ONE

THE UNIQUENESS OF THE WOMAN

EDWIN

For years, I have traveled throughout the world speaking mostly in "men only" meetings. At one conference where I was a guest speaker, the audience was both men and women, and the woman who introduced me saw her opportunity to jibe me humorously about my ministry to men. Her story was:

"God created light and said, 'I can do better,' so He made the worlds. Then He said, 'I can do better,' so He made the animals. He saw the animals and said again, 'I can do better,' so He made man. God saw all He had made and still said, 'I can do better,' so He made woman. Then God rested because He could do no better." We all laughed, but she made her point.

Women are a unique creation of God. Both men and women have a God-given uniqueness, and each is a complement to the other. However, many women have had that uniqueness damaged, changed or perverted in some way and have been robbed, hurt and limited in their womanhood.

For years, women have pressured me to allow them to attend the meetings I have conducted. The meetings are for "men only" simply because a man will respond differently when there are no women present. But the demand from the women became so great, one year I added meetings for "women only" to our schedule. Nancy conducted them, and I spoke and ministered. Literally thousands of women from many backgrounds, cultures, races and persuasions attended meetings held around the world.

Before we began that year of ministry, neither Nancy nor I realized the immensity of the problems, the hurt and the mental, moral, physical and actual trauma done to a woman's sense of uniqueness. It was incredibly rewarding to see the hundreds, truthfully thousands, of women who were helped, changed, and had that blessed sense of uniqueness restored to them during our meetings for "women only."

In America, every fifteen seconds, a woman is beaten.[1] In 1986, a woman was a victim of rape or attempted rape every three and a half minutes. Seventy-seven percent of the victims of violent crimes committed by relatives are women.[2] One out of every four women has been molested. Add to that emotional deprivation, mental abuse, physical neglect and other practices which are rarely reported.

Nancy and I found a wide disparity between women which often stemmed directly from their childhood. Women who had developed a poor self-image from their father's deprecation, abuse or neglect; a mother's dominance; sibling rivalry or animosity; or other assorted familial bruisings, were robbed of their sense of uniqueness and developed abnormal behavior patterns or impaired relationships which lasted until the Lord Jesus Christ renewed them in their uniqueness.

When a woman's uniqueness is plundered, pillaged or ravaged, it can do almost irreparable damage to her and those around her. Women survive but carry the pain, resentment, bitterness and sense of loss with them all through life. Some are emotionally scarred, are mentally disturbed, live with suicidal tendencies or are alienated from society. Most, however, learn to suppress and repress the experiences with the memories and hurt but never enjoy the true freedom of being uniquely a woman.

Psychological help has been a source of relief to help relinquish regret or remorse or ameliorate the suffering. But God has given a way for full restoration of that uniqueness.

A lady once asked me to tell men to send their wives birthday and anniversary cards. She was serious in her request, and I understood why. She wanted to feel unique, to have things that mattered to her be treated with deference and dignity and to know that her husband thought of her as special—therefore honoring her on special occasions.

Everyone, single or married, man or woman, has a recognition hunger that needs to be fed, a thirst for affection that needs to be quenched, a desire for attention that seeks satisfaction.

In speaking to a crowd, when I tell the scenario about a man and woman taking a drive, the story never ceases to elicit a laugh.

He sits behind the wheel of the car which is stopped at a red traffic light. The car is idling and so is he. She sits on her side in quiet contemplation. Suddenly she speaks, "Do you love me?"

To him, her comment is totally irrelevant to the moment. It is extraneous to everything they are engaged in, detached from everything he is thinking and socially inappropriate. So with casual, preoccupied nonchalance, he mutters, "Yeah."

The answer is insufficient to her need, so she asks again, "Do you love me?"

Perturbed, he shoots a look at her and offhandedly says, "I said I did!"

"That isn't what I asked," she says. With a change from soft-spirited hunger to insistent desire, she demands, "I said, 'Do you love me?'"

Putting the car in gear and starting hastily as the light changes to green, he says loudly, "Yes, I said, 'I love you'—OK?"

Sitting straight up in her seat, she says even louder, "All I asked was if you love me, and you start shouting!"

He never answers a word, and for the next twenty minutes, there is a tense silence between them. Finally, he can stand it no longer. He turns to her contritely and says, "Honey, I'm sorry I acted the way I did. Forgive me. I guess the devil just got in there."

The devil didn't have anything to do with it! He was just dumb! All she wanted was a little affection, some personal recognition. She had a desire to have her sense of uniqueness satisfied by personal attention and affection.

If you are a married man reading this book, let me give you a piece of advice. The next time your wife whispers, "Do you love me?" turn to her and say, "Is the sky blue, is water wet, are mountains high? That's how much I love you!" Watch what happens when you give her a loaf of attention instead of tossing her a few crumbs.

Every woman needs love and worth to satisfy her sense of uniqueness. When her worth is only in her body and not in her as a person, tragedy can strike. Hollywood has a graveyard full of stories of such women. Single women know it all too well. Feelings of worthlessness can overwhelm.

While speaking to a group of ministers in Dallas, I told them of the problems ministers' wives suffer. Talking about every person's need for love and worth, I mentioned that many ministers do not understand why their wives are depressed and resent the ministry, them or the congregation.

More often than not, church board members hire a minister, give him a salary, then expect his wife to work in the church as much as the minister. He gets paid, she receives nothing, except maybe an occasional gesture of appreciation that doesn't show her true worth to the church.

Women in the congregation expect her to be at every function, lead women's groups, be attractively coiffed and attired, have her children always dressed perfectly, be a most loving support to her husband and always compliant to the church members' wishes.

Little love, even less worth, makes an unhappy woman.

Looking at those ministers point blank, I told them, "When you don't show your wife love and make ways for the congregation to do it, and when you make her a non-paid volunteer who works as hard as your paid associates, you are looking for trouble.

"Ministers' wives," I continued, "who work in the church alongside their husbands need to feel they are valuable also. Compensate them! Give them a sense of value. Communicate it with gesture, not just with words!"

Two ministers told me later the message changed their marriages. They had never understood their wives' attitudes toward the ministry until then. They never understood before that their own uniqueness was being satisfied by the church, but their wives' uniqueness was not being satisfied at all.

Life must have value or it is worthless!

A biblical understanding of men and women reveals that each derives satisfaction from different sources. Men were created in Adam who was given stewardship over the earth to guide, guard and govern and to oversee the reproduction process on earth by which everything would be replenished after its kind.[3] To this day, a man's uniqueness is basically satisfied in relationship to his job, and his fulfillment comes from the reproduction process involved in it.

The farmer's greatest fulfillment is not in tilling the soil, sowing the seed or watering it, but in the harvest—the reproduction. A salesman's greatest fulfillment is in a satisfied customer. A preacher may begin to grow weary in well doing, but the fulfillment of his ministry rejuvenates him through the reproduction process when a person receives the message and is born of the Spirit of God.

Jesus Himself, when He was wearied with His journey, sat by a well and began conversing with a woman while the disciples went for food. The end result was that He was able to reveal Himself as the Messiah to her, and she believed Him. When the disciples returned, He told them He had "meat to eat that ye know not of."[4] He was replenished in energy by the reproduction process of imparting His revelation and eternal life to her.

Adam had charge of the Garden and he loved God, but God has no peer. Therefore, Adam was "alone," because he had no peer. For love to exist, there must be an object to love. God created woman to be Adam's peer, the object of his love. She was created as a "help meet"[5] or "completer." By creation, she was made to be the completion of the man in God.

God invested Himself in Adam in creation. He breathed into Adam, and Adam became a living soul.[6] He put the Kingdom of God in Adam, and Adam in the Kingdom of God when He placed him in Eden. The characteristics of Adam emanated from the character of God which was inbreathed into him in creation. Adam had the nature of God implanted in him—both the masculine and feminine, tender and tough, disciplinarian and nurturer.

When God created the woman, He took a rib from Adam to make her. The rib was symbolic of something taken from Adam and placed in Eve. If God had created the woman from anything other than that which was already in Adam, He would have created the woman inferior to the man. But God never created any woman to be inferior to any man! Woman was made from man in the beginning, but ever since then, man has come from woman. With this, God shows the equality of men and women.

God took the feminine, the nurturing, the tenderness of His own nature, already inbreathed into Adam, and gave the woman those strengths—leaving the man with the masculine, the disciplinarian, the tough.

Each was and is a God-given strength.

Both man and woman have strengths the world, and each other, needs.

When God created the man, He called him Adam. After He created the woman and brought them into the union of marriage, God called them Adam.[7] She is the complement to the man, and together they make "one" or a "whole."

The man's greatest fulfillment is in the reproduction process, and so is the woman's. A man's uniqueness is basically satisfied in relationship to his job, but a woman's uniqueness is basically satisfied in relationship to a man. A single woman does not have to marry to be "completed," but there is a uniqueness in her that would be satisfied at marriage.

When you begin to understand how God originally created men and women, you begin to comprehend why there are so many difficulties in their relationships.

One problem with marriage is that men and women generally do not recognize or appreciate each other's individuality or uniqueness. They each dream of their ideal then marry the real. The difference between the real and ideal is the degree of disappointment the person feels in the marriage. *Disappointments are not based on what you find but on what you expect to find.*

In dealing with men, I find that many of them do not understand the life principle which requires a man to minister to a woman to make her feel unique to him. They may accidentally do it from time to time, but because they don't understand the principle, they don't make a habit of it.

Courtship is the classic example of this truth.

During courtship, a man generally works hard to convince the lady of his choice that he desires her and her only. She is his exclusive choice to make his life complete. When she is finally convinced, completely sure, she will then agree to marry him.

After marriage, though, he may no longer maintain that attitude, nor attempt to satisfy her uniqueness. Then he wonders why she no longer submits or acts like the woman she "used to be." It is because he no longer seeks to satisfy her sense of uniqueness and simply takes her for granted.

His change begets her change.

The great danger in marriage is when either the husband or the wife begins to demand satisfaction from the other. He cannot demand her submission any more than she can demand his affection. Both must be voluntarily given. Where love is missing, so also are submission and affection.

Today's society puts a heavy burden on both men and women. *Men feel the pressure to perform; women feel the pressure to conform.*

The pressure on a woman to conform comes from every force in society. Her husband may pressure her to conform to his "ideal" of a wife. Consciously or subconsciously, she also feels the pressure from her children, parents and friends to conform to their images of her. In addition, modern media manipulators (called "advertisers") impose their concepts of womanliness with unrelenting pressure—coldly and calculatingly tailoring the concepts in order to sell more of their product. They don't appear to care about the stress in society they create.

It is no wonder women today appear confused, wounded and/or discouraged. Endeavoring to gratify others' expectations frustrates a woman who desires to achieve her own goals in life, to satisfy her own hunger for personal identity or to gain the reward of fulfillment.

Resentment against those who will not accept her as she is will cause a latent hostility which manifests itself in irritability, anger or breakdown. It can be expressed by the cry, "Stop the world, I want to get off!"

God has an answer for that!

God's answer is to please Him first and foremost. By pleasing God, a woman will be pleasing to others, including herself.

There is a rest in the eternal that frees us from the burden of the temporal.

The reason so many women in the Bible followed Jesus, loved Him and ministered to Him is because He so perfectly satisfied their need for uniqueness. He elevated them to the place God originally created them to be by treating them as peers and joint-heirs with Him of their Heavenly Father. He has never changed.

You are unique. God created you to be unique, and where it is impaired, He recreates that uniqueness in your life through Jesus Christ.

NANCY

It was 6 p.m. in Phoenix, Arizona. I glanced at my watch as I checked the ballroom in one of the leading hotels where Edwin and I had scheduled a meeting for women that evening.

I thought, *What woman can attend a meeting at 6:30 p.m. when she works or has to fix dinner, and on a school night, at that?*

But just a few minutes after six, the first women arrived, then more, until, finally, there were several hundred seated in every available chair, eagerly awaiting the ministry that would change some of their lives in ways that, only a few hours before, God alone knew could happen.

At nearly every one of our meetings, Edwin offered prayer at the end of his message for women who had been abused—sexually, physically or otherwise—and he gave the principle of forgiveness from the Bible.

He exhorted them to release out of their lives the resentment, disappointment, bitterness and unforgiveness they felt against the person who wronged them.

That night, again, as we prayed, we saw God do miraculous things in those women. One woman, in particular, stands out in my memory. She was more than 60 years old, tall, stately and graceful, but with a hint of sadness around her eyes and faint, bitter creases down the sides of her mouth.

After prayer, her face moist with fresh tears, she told us that she had been molested as a young girl. Until that night, she had never told anyone. The pain and anguish of the molestation had never left her, she said, although she had managed to live a successful life with the memory carefully tucked away. That evening she publicly voiced her forgiveness for the offender and released the memory, hurt and bitterness of the sin out of her life. Finally, she was free! Her face glowed through the tears, her eyes bright with the love of God.

We returned to our hotel after the meeting, somewhat weary in body but refreshed in spirit. As I lay on my bed before going to sleep, I thought of the very few minutes it had taken God to heal this woman and of the many years she had spent hiding the pain from God as well as everyone else.

What I saw in those meetings were women who really did not know that God is concerned with every area of their lives—areas where they hurt so badly, where they found no relief, where the feelings ran so deeply but they could not share them even with their husbands, parents or anyone close to them.

Their feelings of self-esteem and worth were very low as a result. They asked themselves over and over, "Does God care? Does anyone care? Why should I even care? The knot in my stomach and the band around my emotions are always there! How do I get rid of them? Yes, I am a child of God, but where is the abundant life He promised me?" Finally, they came to an understanding and belief that God cares and will help them.

During a time of crisis in my own life, I asked, "God, when are You going to show Yourself strong on my behalf?"[8]

Well, God *is* faithful. He is a good God. The fact is that many times we are in such a mess, it takes months or even years to straighten us out to the point where He can bless us without our taking advantage of the blessing or misusing it.

I am always amazed and thankful when I see the tremendous power and love that come from the heart of God to restore wounded spirits, bind up the bruised and heal the brokenhearted.[9] Songwriter Charles Gabriel stood "amazed in the presence of Jesus."[10] I echo that phrase when I see people transformed before my eyes. I know that I am one of those transformed people myself.

God loves women! We are His unique creation! Each woman is created to be special. He is as concerned about you as He is about any other woman—or man.

The Bible says, "You were there while I was being formed in utter seclusion! You saw me before I was born and scheduled each day of my life before I began to breathe."[11] God looked at you and said, "Nice work!" and He planned what you would do in your life. Whether or not you are doing it is not just a concern to you but to Him.

The passage goes on to say, "How precious it is, Lord, to realize that you are thinking about me constantly! I can't even count how many times a day your thoughts turn towards me. And when I waken in the morning, you are still thinking of me!"[12] We sometimes believe we need to be thinking about the Lord constantly to be truly "Christian." If our mind wanders, we fear we may have fallen. But the fact is, *He* is thinking about *us* constantly. It is *His* faithfulness that we depend on, not our own.

Even when you first woke up this morning, God was already thinking of you. Hallelujah!

There is no reason why you cannot become all God created you to be. You can be as great as any biblical hero or heroine, but there are obstacles you will have to overcome just as they did. Also, the enemy of your soul—Satan—is real, and if he can convince you that God does not really love you, he can steal your uniqueness as well.

But, if you can become convinced in your heart that God loves you, nothing can stop you from achieving His purposes for your life.

The night of the Phoenix meeting, my faith wavered as I waited for the women to arrive. But what really impressed me is that the women *came*, never minding the inconvenience of the hour or the night, seeking something from the

Lord. I was struck by the purity of purpose they exhibited in seeking God and by a woman who had waited a lifetime for help that had been so readily available to her all along. How many others are there like that?

Never in my wildest dreams did I ever think I would be writing all these thoughts in a book! After many years as a businessman's wife, then a pastor's wife (same man!), as a mother, grandmother and career person—having proved God and found Him always faithful,[13] always the same, never leaving me nor forsaking me[14]—when I was invited to help Edwin with this book, I felt I did have something to share out of a lifetime of experiences, and I wanted to share it with *you*.

CHAPTER TWO

A WOMAN OF GOD

EDWIN

When our present ministry to men began years ago, it sprang from an understanding of truth concerning the nation of Israel as the people left Egypt to enter Canaan. Canaan was the "Promised Land," the place where God wanted Israel to live by faith in order for them to receive the fulfillment of God's promises to them made years before with their forefather, Abraham. It was a place to take joy in God's presence and blessings.

Canaan was a land with the richness of "milk and honey"[1] in contrast to Egypt, which was a place of labor for mere bread and water. Old Testament Canaan was a "type" of New Testament life as recorded in the book of Acts and still lived today. "Canaan," for us, is the reality of a place we enter into by faith in Jesus Christ and through the power of the Holy Spirit. It is a place where we live by faith where His promises are fulfilled and where God is able to make His blessings abound toward us.

However, five sins kept an entire generation of Israelites from entering Canaan and caused them all, except two who were faithful, to die in a wilderness. Those five sins were lust, idolatry, fornication, tempting Christ and murmuring.[2]

The understanding I had and have is that these are the same five sins that keep men today from being maximized in their manhood, prevent marriages from maximizing their potential and prohibit nations from achieving greatness or longevity. After ministering to men for years concerning these truths, I wrote a book entitled *Maximized Manhood*[3] which deals extensively with the subject.

As I mentioned, most of our meetings are basically for men only, so it was interesting when a woman challenged me one day about our ministry. "Why not women in the meetings?" she demanded.

My honest answer was that men act differently when there are no women present. Maybe there is not much that a woman should not hear, but when dealing with subjects like those five sins, I do it very openly and straightforwardly. Then I explained to her how I command men to repent of those sins, and that it might be very uncomfortable for women.

"What makes you think that men are the only ones with those sins?" she shot back at me. "Don't you think women have them also and need to repent?"

She made a good point. We are all subject to the same temptations, identity crises, sins and all have need of Jesus Christ. I discovered recently that the same materials and messages we prepare and present to men are being used by numerous churches which create their women's ministry meetings around them.

Women have always loved to read books we write for men. I caution them, though, that if they read the book first, not to underline it then hand it to their husbands or boyfriends!

I admit it is true. Women need the ministry as much as men. Let's take those same five sins and see how they apply to women.

Lust is perverted love. Lust is the desire to please self even at the expense of others while love desires to please others even at the expense of self.

Women who run up big bills on the credit cards and then protest to their husbands when confronted with the debt, "I did it because I love you," are lying. It is not love; it is lust. Greed is a form of lust. It is the same whether found on Wall Street or in a woman's checkbook.

Gluttony is also lust. Obese women, like men, are generally in that condition because of lustful appetites. An overweight body can keep a woman from a maximized marriage. I will never forget the man in Houston who confided in me after a meeting. He said his wife was attending various prayer meetings, asking for prayer for their marriage, saying it was in dire trouble. She was telling people she did not know what to do with her husband who never showed her any affection.

"Ed," he said, "I love that woman. But she has gained so much weight, she has turned me off. I can't stand to touch her or see her unclothed. There's nothing wrong with our marriage that her losing weight would not cure. I have offered new clothes, a honeymoon trip, paying for diet programs—anything as an incentive to lose weight. But as yet she sees no reason to do it."

I counseled him but never heard the outcome. You must get past the physical to get to the spiritual.[4] A single friend of ours was looking for a man to love her for her Christlike spirit, not her body. But when she received this revelation, she realized she could not disregard her body and expect a man not to notice. When she lost 30 pounds, she was far more attractive, personable, outgoing and became more self-confident with people, which translated into availability and desirability.

Lasciviousness is a form of lust which is living without restraint. It does not make any difference whether lasciviousness is food or sex—it is lust.

There are only three basic temptations: the lust of the flesh, the lust of the eyes and the pride of life.[5] Two-thirds of all temptations in human life comes from lust.

It seems today there is a secondary "ozone layer" made by a spirit of lust that covers the earth. It is like fissionable fallout material that touches everyone everywhere to some degree or another. Soap operas seem to thrive on sex, crime and violence. It seems as if the spirit of television is a spirit of lust. Modern-day romance novels also cater to lustful appetites.

Fornication, or sex sin, is another of the five sins. The Church has not been immune.

Sex sins have been the problem of the Church since the 1980s.

Women serving as temple prostitutes are not found just in the Old Testament,[6] but they are a New Testament affliction of the Church as well. Of course, we are too nice, too enlightened and sophisticated, too couth and cultured, too religious to admit that the women we read about, who are having affairs with ministers, are oftentimes nothing more than temple prostitutes. They lust after men of God rather than seek God and, oftentimes, are thinking that they are doing God "service" by servicing men of God.

Lesbianism among women leaders in the world today also has had an effect on all society.

Once a deeply distressed man wanted to talk to me for counsel. He was suffering terribly since his wife left him. When he told me she had run off with one of their best friends, I asked, "What was he like?"

He whispered, "It wasn't a he."

Talk about the emasculation of manhood in the world today! He was experiencing it firsthand. Losing your wife to another man is not uncommon but losing her to another woman is devastating.

The same devastation can come from homosexuality. What must it be like for the woman whose husband "comes out of the closet," confesses he is homosexual, insists he can be bisexual, states he wants to continue the marriage and wants her to share his love with another man? How damnably selfish!

It was hard for me to come to grips with the fact that women have sexual addictions that are as strong as or stronger than men's. The world's "Chippendale" syndrome is a reality—fanatically addicted women worshipping the male phallus, willing to lose all virtue and, without shame, succumbing to their basest lusts.

The great deception of our day is thinking you can practice an immoral lifestyle and still be in right relationship with God. No one who abides in Christ can habitually practice sin.[7]

To say you cannot live without abiding in sin is to deny the power of the Resurrection. The Spirit of Holiness that raised Christ from the dead can still enable men and women to lead "overcoming" lives.

There is a difference between someone who commits a sin and someone who practices sin. Whether the sex sin is an image of the mind, a perverted philosophy that justifies a moral aberration or an unclean habit, it needs to be admitted, confessed, repented of and forsaken.

If you committed a sex sin, ask God to forgive you, and when you know He has—then forgive yourself, forsake that way, and live a life pleasing to God.

As a brother stated at one of our meetings, *"You don't drown by falling in the water—you drown by staying there!"*

Tempting Christ is to insist or demand that God do what is contrary to His Word, inconsistent with His will or foreign to His way. To continue to live in known sin is a form of tempting Christ, as is asking God's blessing on a wedding day when you know not to marry the man. Men and women both must repent of tempting Christ.

Idolatry is another of the five sins. "A woman's home is her security" is an old adage, but a home can be an idol and the possessions, fetishes. A "way of life" can also be idolatrous, and has been, to more than one woman's hurt.

Women who want to be a man's idol, to have him "put her on a pedestal," choose a hard life. A pedestal is just as much a prison as any other small space.

Pornography, "hard porn" or "soft porn," is actually idolatrous, not just lustful. Mental images created in the mind become idols, and habitual masturbation becomes an act of worship.

Murmuring is another sin which kept Israel from Canaan and keeps women today from entering their "Promised Land." Faultfinding, backbiting, criticizing, nagging, gossiping are all forms of murmuring. Precious friendships have been lost from "cattiness," which is nothing but another form of murmuring.

The Israelites complained to Moses about the difficult journey they were taking. They chafed under the commandments and cried about the "angel food" (manna)[8] God provided for them to eat. God viewed their complaints to Moses as a sin against Him and punished them accordingly.

Single women complaining about their lot in life, the absence of available men and the hardship and loneliness of being single need to take heed to themselves lest they be found murmuring against God for their way of life. If they are not careful, they will die in a wilderness of despair or die from the poison in the root of bitterness sown in their hearts.

Murmuring keeps many women from enjoying the blessings of God.

I shall never forget the minister in Pittsburgh, Pennsylvania, who told me how his life had almost been destroyed. He had a woman parishioner to whom he was attracted, but he took no action except to entertain thoughts about her. He knew even this was wrong and, in a godly attempt to cleanse his mind and heart, went to a fellow minister to confess his fault "one to another."[9]

After the session with his minister friend, he stopped to visit someone in a hospital, went by his office and then went home. As he stepped inside his front door, he saw his wife posed belligerently before him.

"Tell me all about it, you adulterer!" she shot at him balefully. Their relationship degenerated from that point, and it had still not recovered when he told me about it years later. The minister's friend told his wife about the minister's confession, who, in turn, called the minister's wife to tell her, and the rest is history.

Gossip is murmuring. Pastors contend that one of the worst problems they face, and one that can destroy ministries quicker than anything else, is gossip in the church. Women who attend prayer meetings and profess concern for others, often make prayer requests which, in reality, are a pious form of gossip.

A young wife who had an extramarital affair genuinely repented and earnestly endeavored to put her marriage back together through the grace of God. But she found it very difficult, because those in whom she confided, who she thought would help counsel her, actually hindered her by passing from person to person the news about her escapade in a "sympathetic sister syndrome." It was really a form of slander, and slander is murmuring. It is also criminal.

I am not saying anything that I have not already said in person and in writing to more than five million men. But now I am saying it to you. Murmuring is a sin!

Single, married, widowed, divorced—all women face areas of life where they need to overcome temptations and sins, leave them behind and enter their "Promised Lands." I am challenging you to do exactly that.

Show yourself a woman!

Several years ago, during a meeting in Constitution Hall in Washington, D.C., there came a moment when the joy of the Lord came up in me with exuberant enthusiasm. In the exhilaration of the moment, I took off my coat, flung it around my head in an arc, and shouted, "I am not ashamed to say I want to be a man of God."

Astonishingly, within seconds, that entire crowd was standing to its feet, and two thousand men strong were shouting the same thing. Boldness is a form of courage.

In every Christlike life, there needs to be a time, or times, when an uninhibited, enthusiastic, God-glorifying declaration of heartfelt desire is entered into in a righteous way. "Praise is comely for the upright."[10]

A "laid-back" culture finds such behavior objectionable, but God does not. In fact, God Himself spoke with a loud voice, saying, "This is my beloved Son, in whom I am well pleased."[11] And Jesus sometimes prayed with a loud voice.[12]

When it comes to Christianity, identification is the basic issue. Knowledge of who you are in Christ is edifying. There is nothing more thrilling than to stand in the righteousness of God and declare your identity with Christ. Men have no copyright on that.

Try it! *A healthy dose of courage is like medicine to the soul.*

NANCY

I want to continue the subject Edwin brought up about identity—now that I have declared, "I am not ashamed to say I want to be a woman of God!"

Recently, I read a magazine article about women creating their "identity" with clothes. As I read, I thought, *If I create my identity with clothes that are put on and taken off, where is the real me?* For one thing, I'm not always going to be wearing the right clothes. I might be in an old robe or wearing the wrong color!

The search for "identity" became an issue during the heyday of the modern women's movement. Women entered an "identity crisis" as they rebelled at the standards others imposed on them. One popular solution to the identity crisis was to substitute a career for a husband and children. But later, women who skipped having babies in their twenties began to have children in their thirties and older. Also, many women bent on climbing ladders of success, or "finding" themselves at the expense of others, failed in their relationships at home and at work. Other avenues of "finding one's identity" were just as futile.

One of the definitions of *identity* is "the condition or fact of being the same or exactly alike; sameness; oneness; groups united by *identity* of interests." Another is "individuality."[13]

To me, identity means being the same inside and out. Identities based on style, careers, husbands, children or lack thereof, do not provide true "identity" because they are changeable aspects of life. We also are constantly changing.

The issue is deeper than what we do, with whom we associate or what we wear. If "identity" means to be the same as something, we can find it only in something outside ourselves that does not change. If we try to find our identities in our husbands or through our jobs, we lose our own uniqueness by conforming to something else, something as changeable as we are.

There is, however, One Who is absolute, Who never changes, and that is Jesus Christ. He is "the same yesterday, and today, and for ever."[14] He was there when we were created, knows our purpose in life and knows who we are in our heart of hearts. He alone knows the real "me" far better than I know myself.

How do you find your identity in Christ? You find it by allowing Him to show you your own heart, then by purifying your heart so that you become the same, inside and out.

A friend made a very astute statement one day. She said, "You cannot give a soulish answer to a spiritual problem." Trying to "find yourself" outside the spirit realm will never provide the identity you are seeking and, therefore, will never result in the peace and fulfillment you can find through Christ.

I know a few people who seem to have completely solved their identity crises. One of them, a well-known Bible teacher, told a congregation one day about her struggles for a pure heart.[15] She said that, as a child, she determined to be thoroughly Christlike. After marriage, she came to the conclusion that of all the aspects of herself, the mind was the hardest to be purified. So she went through an intense time of seeking God.

Her daily goal became this: "When my husband comes home from work, I want to feel as though I could write all my thoughts of the day on a blackboard and not be ashamed of them."

As a member of that congregation, I was so impressed by her statement that I can still hear her voice in my mind. The goal seemed completely unattainable and yet so worthy. I began to see that as we are thoroughly purified, we are also thoroughly identified with Jesus. We lose our identity in Him. And by losing our identities, we find them.[16]

This is difficult to do, and all of us fail at times, but I have learned, first of all, that even when I fail, God is faithful.[17] Secondly, I have learned that at the times of greatest intimacy with the Lord, I am most "myself," inside and out. Everything I ever thought I could be, those God-given desires, seem to surface. The Holy Spirit gives me courage to attempt them, and God is faithful to help me succeed. But the things which were my own wishful thinking, or negative thoughts, vanish in the light of God's presence within me.

For years, I felt the stress of an "identity crisis." Frequently, I found myself wanting to be what I thought my family, friends or others wanted me to be.

At each of the five different churches Edwin and I pastored, I felt pressure to be a certain kind of woman. In our first pastorate, the women thought I would easily lead the intercessory prayer group. What they did not know was that I had been a Christian a scant two years, and I knew almost nothing about intercessory prayer.

But what did I do? I tried to lead the group! Somehow, that weekly meeting dissolved, and I hardly noticed it. I did not even know, at the time, the importance of intercessory prayer.

In another church, we had very few people. In fact, on our first Sunday, the entire congregation was one lady and her baby! As the church grew, I was asked to do anything and everything, qualified or not. I was a Sunday School teacher for various grades, sang in the choir, led the choir, conducted Children's Church, counseled and so forth.

In some areas, I sometimes performed well, so I kept trying different avenues of service from church to church, feeling obligated to do so. But that chameleon-like existence finally had to end if I were to find my true purpose and identity in Christ. Finally, through some good teaching, I found what my talents and strengths were, and I quit striving to be something I was not. I could sing in the choir but not lead it. I could organize women's ministries but not necessarily teach them. I could share my own experiences with different groups and have always been comfortable with personal witnessing but could never face a crowd as an evangelist.

But these are pressures from only one area of life. There are other pressures—from family, media and other sources—that confront us daily. I have found that the more we are identified with Christ, the more freedom we have from the pressures of people's images of us. The more we stabilize ourselves in Him, the more we can transcend circumstances and stresses.

Some people may be surprised to find that identifying with Jesus is as much a woman's privilege as a man's. But the Apostle Paul teaches in the Bible that in God's Kingdom, there is neither "Jew nor Greek...bond nor free...male nor female."[18] Jesus came to earth for both men and women. He longs for that deep, intimate friendship with both men and women. There is only one faith.[19] We are joined together, male and female, by our faith in Jesus, Who is our hope of glory.[20]

If you are not familiar with the Bible, at first, it may seem to be a "man's book" because of all the stories about men. Those men are examples for us women, just as are the stories of women.[21] When women depersonalize the Scriptures by attributing their relevance only to men, they have to seek elsewhere to find what they are supposed to do in relationship to God. They may begin to prefer books and teachings over personal study of the Word. As a result, many women do not aspire to the higher things of God and often miss out on what God intends for their lives.

I thank God for teachers, authors and ministers who have enriched my life with their revelations from God and with their life experiences, but I know I cannot substitute their teachings for in-depth Bible study and prayer. The standard of measure for every woman's life is the Word of God. The goal for every woman's life is Christlikeness. It is good to study how Sarah submitted, but Christ's submission to the Father is our greatest example. It is good to study the intercession of Abigail with David,[22] but Christ's intercession for us[23] is our greatest example.

The Word of God and the Holy Spirit living within us will teach us daily and lead us into a closer relationship with the Father which will bring us into our true identities.

Jesus can solve every identity crisis.

CHAPTER THREE

SEIZE THE OPPORTUNITY!

NANCY

Some time ago, I began thinking about opportunities God might give me to be of service to Him. He brought to life for me the story of Abigail. She was "a woman of good understanding, and of a beautiful countenance," but she was married to a man named Nabal who was "churlish and evil in his doings."[1]

While hiding from Saul, David and his men protected Nabal's shepherds and flocks. David and his men were like "a wall" to them which indicates protection.[2] In return, they asked Nabal for the kindness of feeding them when they were hungry. Nabal, being rich, easily could have provided for them. However, he refused, saying he didn't even know who they were. As a result, David determined to kill Nabal and every man in his household.

When Nabal's men told Abigail, she immediately took a supply of food to David and apologized for her husband's behavior. Abigail saw what her husband was blind to—that David was God's man.[3] She appealed for her husband's life and turned David's wrath away from her household.

When Abigail told Nabal what had happened, his heart "became as a stone," and within ten days, he was dead.[4] When David heard of Nabal's death, he sent for Abigail and married her. In exchanged for Abigail's act of courage in a moment of need, she became one of the wives of a future king of Israel. Abigail seized the opportunity to do something for the Lord, and, as a result, she was rescued from a terrible marriage and elevated to one of the highest positions a woman could have in that day.

Another story that struck me with fresh revelation was that of Ruth who made the choice to follow God and ended up being part of the lineage of Christ.[5] Ruth, a Moabite, was married to an Israelite. After his death, she chose to return to Israel with her mother-in-law and serve her mother-in-law's God rather than remain in Moab with pagan gods.

Later, she married Boaz, a kinsman of her late husband, and became the great-grandmother of David, who was a direct ancestor of Jesus. She seized an opportunity and made a mark in history.

I had known the stories of these two women for years without realizing the importance of their examples.

For years, I had said, "No, thank you, I am not a speaker," whenever I was asked to address a group. I knew I was not one of the great speakers of our day, although God had used me in that area once or twice.

But the Apostle Paul admonished us to "Walk in wisdom toward them that are without, redeeming the time,"[6] which also means, "make the most of every opportunity."[7] I had let opportunities slip by based on the mistaken conviction that I had nothing to say. I was comfortable with letting Edwin take the lead and knew I was in God's will by supporting him.

Then God showed me there were times when I hid behind Edwin's accomplishments and did not do everything of which I was capable. God gently revealed to me that some of my "hanging back" and being a "silent partner" was not only a lack of faith on my part, but also

SEIZE THE
OPPORTUNITY!

a laziness of spirit and complacency that said, "I have enough of God's blessings; I don't need any more."

From living with a minister, I knew doing more for the Lord—such as speaking or writing a book—required more prayer, more Bible study and a lot more walking in the Spirit, not the flesh. Also, I thought, *What if God does not bless my efforts?* Talk about a lack of faith!

At one time, I had taken on obligations in areas that were not really "me," but now I found I was not seizing the opportunities that really were for me.

It is not always easy doing God's work—but think about Abigail. What would have become of her and her household if she had not seized the opportunity to do the right thing when it presented itself?

A close friend of mine years ago was able to entertain for the church, work in the women's ministries and give to the poor, but she would never speak up for Jesus. She thought she was not qualified, so she missed God's blessings. The shame is that she was extremely personable and articulate talking about almost any other subject, but she let Satan blind her in this one area.

When we let Satan blind us, there is always a little nagging in our spirits and a void there. If we stop to listen, a still small voice would be telling us to get up and seize opportunities in front of us, to look for the hidden or unseen talents and abilities in our lives that could be used for the Lord.

Obey that gentle, "still small voice."[8] Really, it is the Holy Spirit, not our own crazy thoughts. God says in His Word that His gentleness will make us great.[9] So keep your ears open for God's gentle voice. He wants to maximize your life and mine just as He did Abigail's and Ruth's.

Commit and submit your talents, dreams and desires to God. Let Him sanctify you, then seize those opportunities He makes available to you.

Why do more women not rise to greatness? There are women who are familiar with the lives of all the great women achievers in the Bible, yet they still believe they themselves have no such traits. This belief permeates their whole lives so they do not fulfill their potential.

Perhaps they believe men are smarter than women. I have news for those who believe this—cultural issues aside—they are not! A recent article in the *Los Angeles Times* newspaper written by March C. Linn, professor of Education at the University of California, Berkeley, and psychologist Janet S. Hyde of the University of Wisconsin, found that men's verbal proficiency has been increasing during the last twenty years to match women's, while women's mathematical abilities have been increasing to match men's. The researchers concluded, "The differences are now so small as to be negligible. We should de-emphasize this issue."[10]

You have more than you think you have.

You can do more than you think you can.

You alone are responsible to use the intelligence, talents, abilities and gifts God has given to you. They just need cultivation.

Remember, when Moses spoke to the assembly of Israel, men and women, he said, "Be strong and of a good courage."[11] And Jesus said to both men and women, "Be of good cheer; I have overcome the world."[12] The Lord spoke through the Prophet Joel, "Your sons and your *daughters* shall prophesy... upon the *handmaids*...will I pour out my spirit."[13]

God does not give women all those spiritual blessings to keep to themselves. He gives them to edify others, to enrich His Kingdom and to accomplish His purposes through us.

The Prophet Isaiah wrote, "Rise up, ye women that are at ease; hear my voice, ye careless daughters!"[14] That is what I had to do. I had to "rise up" to fulfill God's purpose, not only in my life but in the lives of others whom I touched and influenced. "Rising up" was part of spiritual growth, of becoming a mature Christian and of becoming an overcomer.

Another thing that stops women from seizing opportunities is simply the lack of courage to overcome. Women who refuse to be spiritual overcomers get overcome by others. Wicked men find their way into the homes of "weak-willed women,"[15] preying on them and making their lives a hell on earth. Women make weak decisions and become slaves to their own choices.[16] That is no way to live.

The life of an overcomer is the life to live!

Deborah was an overcomer whose deeds are recorded in the Bible. While serving as a judge in Israel, she motivated General Barak to achieve his greatest victory by promising to go with him into battle. That took courage. As a result, the Bible says, poetically, "They ceased in Israel, until that I Deborah arose, that I arose a mother in Israel."[17]

Esther's is yet another remarkable story of courage that overcomes.[18] Many Israelites of the tribe of Judah were exiled into Persia during her day. All of them, including Esther, were scheduled to be slaughtered, even though Esther, from all of the king's wives, had been made queen. Esther's godly cousin, Mordecai, encouraged her to approach the king about their impending doom; however, no one, not even the queen, was allowed to go to the king without an invitation. If she petitioned the king and he did not hold out his scepter toward her, she would be executed.

So Esther had Mordecai and her people fast and pray for three days with her before she approached the king. The end result was that she found favor with the king, her people were saved, and Mordecai was elevated to one of the highest positions in the land. Through her, the Israelites were given a powerful voice in government, even though they were a conquered nation living in exile in a foreign land.

The midwives who saved Israelite babies in Egypt centuries before Esther had also been courageous. Their courage allowed Moses to live and grow up to lead their people out of bondage to the "Promised Land." Ordered to kill all the baby boys, instead, these women hid them from Pharaoh and protected them. God saved the lives of the midwives and, as a reward, provided houses for them.[19]

There are opportunities everywhere for women who have the courage to seize them. In addition to church and Christian work, there are jobs, hobbies, charity work and businesses you can start on your own. God puts desires in your heart so that He may fulfill them.[20]

You need not shrink from any position, even one in which you will be managing others. Mothering is a form of managing, and that is something we women are uniquely qualified to do. Deborah led ten thousand men with Barak. Her strength came from her wisdom, from her knowledge of God and from knowing His will for her life. Stability—the ability to stand your ground—comes with wisdom, knowledge and the strength of your salvation.[21]

If you need more wisdom, simply ask for it from God, "Who gives generously" without making you feel guilty for asking![22]

When a woman has a desire to achieve and aspires to more than the women around her, often she is labeled a "feminist." However, if she puts God first, family second, and allows God to set the rest of her priorities, then it does not matter how much she attains, she is still walking with God.

One woman leader whom I admire is Margaret Thatcher, former Prime Minister of Great Britain. Her ability to run a nation and her household and still take time for her grandchildren was a great inspiration to me. She is considered to have been one of the most successful leaders in the world and, in some circles, the most successful. Yet, as one newspaper columnist points out,[23] instead of lauding her successes as a career woman, "feminists" tend to ignore her, possibly because she is also a happily married woman, mother and grandmother, and she appears to have no hatred of men.

There is a balance to be found between aggressive and weak-willed women. The Apostle Paul had to teach about striking a balance where women were concerned. Jesus' attitude and teachings were, and are, extremely liberating to people, but they especially were to women of that day.

Paul taught about our freedom in Christ but warned not to use that freedom as an occasion for evil.[24]

The same is true for us today. Your freedom to achieve, to seize opportunities and to strive to be all that you can be does not give you the freedom to run over other people or to move in opposition to authority or to God. Edwin has more on this subject.

EDWIN

Christlikeness and womanhood are synonymous.

The basic quality in womanhood is femininity.

Femininity has as much strength as masculinity. Each is manifested in different ways.

When women try to compete with men by emulating men, they abandon their own strengths and attempt to win in a competition that becomes unequal.

Lois is our middle child. It was Lois who announced to me on a "700 Club" television program that she was pregnant with her first child. I fell off my chair while Ben Kinchlow, the host, laughed uproariously.

Once, when she was fourteen years old, she objected one afternoon to what her mother wanted her to do. Her mother made her do it, and afterward, Lois entered her bedroom and closed the door on the family. When dinner time came, I made her come to the table although she remonstrated. I wanted to change her attitude, so I asked her to say grace.

She gave me a hard look, slowly looked at each member of the family, then bowed her head to pray: "Lord, I thank You that You have prepared a table before me in the presence of mine enemies."

We all laughed so hard we could barely eat. Today Lois is a prosecuting attorney in a district attorney's office in California. Recently, a hardened, experienced defense attorney met her in the hallway and paid her a very high compliment.

"Lois," he said, "I want to commend you on your skills. You are one woman I never want to meet in court. You are doing exactly what I would do if I were a woman—you dress and act like a lady in court. You are smart."

That is not the only reason she has been hard to beat, but it is a good reason, and she admits it. When she once tried to compete as a man, at the behest of her superiors, she lost the first case of her career. That was her last loss for several years. She learned a tough lesson. She needs the strengths of her womanhood. Laying aside her femininity and taking on a masculine demeanor weakened her ability.

Women are great achievers.

Three of the greatest world leaders since World War II have been women: Golda Meir of Israel, Indira Gandhi of India and Margaret Thatcher of Great Britain.

However, some men hide behind strong women. Some women are just quicker, smarter and more talented than the men they are married to. A woman like that needs to be careful not to usurp her husband's role.

In Honolulu, in front of a large church audience where several dozen couples had come forward for prayer, I questioned them regarding why they were there.

"Are you Navy?" I asked one young man standing hand-in-hand with his wife.

Before he could answer, she said, "Yes, he is."

My next question was, "How long have you been married?"

Again, she answered for him, "Five years."

Then she volunteered, "We have been separated for seven months and just got back together a month ago."

I studied them for a minute. He stood with his head down, his free hand clenched, jaw muscles working. She stood next to him, pretty, innocent-looking and with wide-eyed eagerness, ready to answer every question.

"I am talking to him—let him answer," I said to her gently.

After he answered a few questions, I told them, as politely as I knew how, the problem facing them.

"You are quick, bright and fast on the trigger," I told her. "Your husband is slower, thinks before he speaks and is very deliberate. You are impatient with him. You want to quicken the pace. You find it difficult to wait for him to make decisions. He lets you do it but resents it. He defers to you but knows he should not. You are both wrong.

"Impatience is the tool of the flesh and misunderstanding the tool of the devil. You are playing into the hands of both. Unless you both change, you will part again."

If one spouse is impatient with the other, discontentment sets in, and then it becomes almost impossible to see the good traits and strengths of the other. And, "A brother offended is harder to be won than a strong city."[25]

A strong woman can make a man morally lazy. He lets her do it all and absolves himself of his responsibility in decision making. There are women who delight in this, though. They want to have a world where they are queens and men are serfs, subservient to every whim of the woman. This is a "Jezebel" spirit. Jezebel, King Ahab's wife in the Bible, was in competition with men. She rebelled against society's mores, seduced men to false religious worship, denied God's sovereignty, corrupted a nation, polluted people's spirits, controlled her husband and, with an adulterous spirit, abrogated to herself control of a country.[26]

That same spirit is prevalent in our land today.

A man in ministry who has a strong and assertive wife can do very well as long as the man retains the authority of leadership. When the wife assumes the authority, the husband loses his ability to lead. Women are not to usurp authority from male leadership.[27]

There is strong controversy to this day over women in ministry. However, some of the greatest women I know are in ministry. But there is danger when women do not recognize divine order.

One woman minister I know came to grief because of this. She was personable, knew the Word of God and had a gift of teaching. People loved her, and soon she was in demand outside her local church. She accepted the invitations gladly and with her husband's blessing.

Her ministry expanded. She was immensely satisfied in her work. There was appreciation, recognition, affection from the people to whom she ministered. But the perception she had of herself soon shifted from the priority of being wife and mother to being a peer with men in ministry.

Imperceptibly, she began to be more and more irritable with her husband, tended to neglect her responsibilities to her family and did not recognize the loss of intimacy in her marriage. At the same time, she began to develop a great affinity for a male prayer partner.

She failed to recognize there are both positive and negative aspects in the principle that prayer produces intimacy. In the positive, intimacy in spirit between married people can be carried into sexual relations. More than one marriage with sexual difficulties has been healed when the couple began to pray together consistently.

But when prayer partners who are not married develop such an intimacy, fornication or adultery can result. That is the negative. For this reason, a single Christian woman will often have difficulty breaking off a wrong relationship with a man. Her prayer for him maintains a degree of intimacy that makes it difficult not to want to be with him.

The woman minister ultimately entered into an adulterous affair with her prayer partner. It seemed so right to her. But it was so wrong! The discovery of their affair led to her loss of a ministry, a prayer partner and, almost, a family.

Sin is so deceptive.

Gifts and anointings are no substitute for obedience. She seized her opportunity but forgot her authority.

That is why there has to be a chapter on submission.

CHAPTER FOUR

THERE HAS TO BE A CHAPTER ON SUBMISSION

EDWIN

Submission is God's plan for restoration.

Submission is meant to liberate, not put in bondage.

However, due to the misunderstanding and misapplication of the principle, it has been perverted into something other than God's original purpose. Error oftentimes is nothing but truth carried to the extreme.

Literally thousands of marriages have problems because husbands and wives do not understand this principle of the Kingdom.

Submission is God's method of revealing His "transcendent glory" in the restoration process. His transcendent glory is His ability to take things meant for evil and convert them to work for our good when they are submitted and committed to Him.

An excellent example of God's transcendent glory is found in the biblical story of the people living on the plain of Shinar who decided to build a tower to Heaven. They were all of one language, one mind and one heart. By making a name for themselves, it was their intention to establish themselves as gods. When God saw their unity, He knew they would be able to complete the construction project.[1]

In His wisdom, God confounded their languages. The use of tongues produced powerlessness and division when they no longer could speak the same language. Through that strategy, He rendered them helpless and incapable of finishing the tower.

Centuries later, after His resurrection and before He ascended into Heaven, Jesus told His disciples to "wait for the promise of the Father."[2] He had prayed the Father to send the Holy Spirit into their lives, and when the Father answered, Jesus wanted the disciples ready to receive it.

The followers gathered in an "upper room"[3] in obedience to His command, and after ten days of purification, there came a manifestation of the Spirit of God.[4] All of them began to speak in languages they had never learned. At that moment, God used tongues to unite the believers and release the power of His Spirit in their lives.

At the tower of Babel, tongues, and the lack of agreement they produced, resulted in powerlessness. In the upper room, tongues, and the agreement of the believers gathered, resulted in a release of power.

God took what was meant for a curse in Old Testament days and turned it into a blessing in New Testament living.

God did the same with submission. From the beginning of creation until sin entered the world, Adam and Eve lived as joint-heirs. Jointly, they inherited the blessing of God and exercised dominion over the earth.[5] After their denial of God's sovereignty, when the curse came as a result of their sin, Eve was told Adam would have the "rule" over her.[6] The evidence and result of this can be seen historically in society where women were, and are, treated as "second-class citizens."

Jesus Christ, "the last Adam," came to redeem us from the curse of sin[7] resulting from the first Adam's sin and restore us to God's original purpose, which is for man and woman to live as "joint-heirs." Submission, which was part of the curse in the Old Testament, became God's method of restoring woman to a joint-heirship with her husband in the New Testament. A woman's submission before Christ was involuntary as the result of the curse. Now, after Christ, her submission is a voluntary expression of faith.

Submission to the pastor, father, teacher or any other authority is actually an act of faith. When a wife submits to her husband's authority, she puts herself voluntarily, by faith, into divine order[8] and gives the man the ability to treat her as a joint-heir. Rebellion causes him to resort to "ruling," not "leading."

A woman does not receive God's grace in salvation through any man, for Christ is her Savior and the Captain of her salvation. In marriage, even though Christ is still her Savior and Head of her life, the man is head of the house. Her submission to her husband shows her submission to her Lord.

If a woman submits to her husband, and he does not treat her as God commands, then he is sinning against God, and his prayers will not get ready answers.[9] God will not hear the man who has iniquity in his heart when he prays.[10] A man's disregard, domination or demeaning of his wife is iniquitous in the sight of God.

However, the nuances of submission are many and varied in practice. A young couple whose marriage was in distress poured out their problems to me one day in my office. She talked the most, repeatedly saying that all she wanted was to be his wife, to love him and be intimate with him in every way. She was willing to leave her job, go to work in his office full time instead of occasionally and do whatever she could to be close to him.

In earnest, she confessed how mystified she was that, with all her efforts, he shut her out of his life, and there was little intimacy between them. Her desire was intense, and she feared most of all that he would turn to other women.

When both of them had disclosed everything they wanted to and were ready to receive counsel, I started by speaking to her. I was direct.

"Your husband does not want you at work with him for a reason," I began. "You have a habit of second-guessing him, which, in essence, is making his decisions for him. At home, he tolerates it and says nothing. In the office, it is *seditious*. His authority is undermined, and he is embarrassed, emasculated, and he resents it.

"Rather than telling you how he feels, he avoids the conflict and confrontation by keeping you out of the office. You feel 'shut out' because you *are* being shut out. I do not want to offend you, but your behavior takes on a form of murmuring and lacks submission.

"In the office, his secretary does what he says, supplies the details for him as needed, whether it is ordering lunch or statistics, and makes suggestions only to help—not to challenge his authority. You want intimacy, but you are creating distance. He has built barriers as defenses against your intrusion into his territory.

"What happens in cases like this is what you suspect to be happening: the secretary becomes more intimate than the wife because the secretary and boss share everything at the office, but the wife and husband are not doing the same at home. When that happens, secretaries become 'office wives.' They give the man everything but sex. And if the intimacy at home does not match the intimacy at the office, the secretary may eventually give him sex, too."

It was tough. Love is tough. Speaking the truth in love heals, not wounds. Truth may be hard to swallow—but then, most medicines are.

Motives are hard to discover at any time, which is why the Word of God is so necessary in our lives. The sharpness of the Word can divide between motives, intentions and actions.[11]

We believe there has to be a chapter on submission in this book, but there is an entire book of truth on the subject, and that is the Bible. The Bible does not speak of male dictatorship but of male leadership.

The two most common questions we receive in letters from women are:

"How can I get my husband to take the lead in the home?"

And, "How can I get my husband to pray with me?"

Only God can provide the solution to every problem created by man. We are limited, but His wisdom is available to all.[12]

Once while I was sitting in a pastor's office, waiting for a meeting, a young couple came in and introduced themselves to me. Carl was a big bulwark of blue-collar bravado, and his wife, Elizabeth, was a tall, lanky, red-haired hair stylist with the gift of gab. All things considered, they looked like a pretty even match for a fight. According to them, they had participated in many "rounds" through the years.

Knowing me through my books, they began to tell of the changes in their lives that had led to a wonderful marriage. They explained that, for the past two years, their marriage had become something of rare and precious value to them both.

They had been on the brink of divorce when Elizabeth turned to God in desperation and began to cry out for wisdom. She could see Carl's faults and flaws so clearly but could not see how to turn him around to behave more reasonably. She was living and conducting herself in marriage through what she had learned from her mother, but now she was asking her Heavenly Father.

She began to search for answers in *The Amplified Bible*. First, when she read Ephesians 5:33, she discovered that she was to respect her husband, regardless of his faults. Then she saw if she expected him to change, she would have to submit to him, according to 1 Peter 3:1. These two verses became the foundation for her life and the basis of her faith and conduct. Taking them very much to heart, she began to put the Word into action. Both were contrary to her natural inclinations, but she knew obedience to the Word was God's only method of protection for her life.

She began to work on herself, using the Word as a mirror. Instead of a pattern of resistance and insistence, she deliberately chose one of submission through love. At times humiliated, depressed, frustrated and angry, Elizabeth persisted. She admitted there were moments when she felt like giving in or giving up, and there were other occasions when she thought she would die. Now she realizes the only way to live a resurrected life *is* by way of death, death to self.

Through much prayer and conscientious follow-through, a supernatural change took place in her attitudes, habits, thought and speech patterns and in her relationship to Carl. But the transition was so natural, it was hardly noticeable. The changes in her prompted changes in him. He not only took the lead, but he began to pray with her as well.

As I stood up for my meeting, Carl had the last word and briefly summed up his feelings. "I can never do enough for her. Honestly, Ed, for me it is a thrill to be able to bless her and do things that give her joy."

They had entered their "Promised Land."

This is just one example of the many nuances of submission. Nancy has more.

NANCY

Submission is the Word of God in action. If we can believe the Bible to save our souls, why do we have such difficulty in believing its teachings on submission? I have heard or read many, many different viewpoints on the subject. But, first of all, let's make it clear that submission is *not* just a word for women!

Yesterday I went to the post office and got stuck behind nine other people. Only one person worked the desk, and then he, too, disappeared! Those of us waiting were talking among ourselves, not being very complimentary of the way our small town post office was being run. However, like it or not, we had to *submit* to what was going on because it was the only post office we could use. That is basic submission.

Being willing to let others stand in front of you because they were there first is submission. Have you ever been waiting at the grocery store when a new checkout stand opens next to yours and the clerk motions to the person behind you, even though you have been waiting longer? That is submission. (Unless you make a scene!)

To some women, submission is a dirty, ten-letter word. In reality, submission is simply a fact of life. Submission is not some cruel act committed against women. It is a principle of business, government and school. In fact, everywhere you look, the principle of submission is at work.

For example, what color are your eyes? One gene had to submit to another to make that color. The earth submits to the rays of the sun. We submit to the government, we submit to traffic signals, and we submit to authorities every day. We might not like those to whom we submit. And yet, to be truly Christlike, we must be submissive. That is why the Apostle Paul admonished Christians to submit to authorities and to one another, men and women both.[13]

We do not just submit upwardly, either. Often we end up submitting to our own children in order to let them learn something for themselves. What else can it be when, after saying "hot" for two years, you finally let your toddler get close enough to the stove to feel the heat and decide for himself to withdraw his hand?

But let's take a look at the biblical basis for a woman's submission to her husband, which is found in Ephesians 5:21-25. First, both men and women are admonished to submit to one another, which, to me, means, "esteem and look upon and be concerned...each for the interests of others."[14] Submission is an attitude of heart which should be prevalent in both women and men.

Ephesians 5:22-24 states that a wife is to submit to her husband. As she submits, she carries out the attitude of humility, recognizing his authority as the head of the family.

But then the very next verse (v. 25) was stated almost in the same breath: "Husbands, love your wives, even as Christ loved the church, and gave himself for it." An awesome responsibility rests on both the husband and the wife, and each is accountable to God for obedience to His Word.

Christian wives are called to submit to their husbands, but that is not their greatest calling! Their greatest calling is to live a Christlike life, and that is the aspect of Christianity that we emphasize.

Submission to God takes precedence over submission to anyone and anything else.[15] Remember when Israel wanted a king? They wanted one to avoid submitting to God.[16] They erred by trying to avoid their individual responsibility to God.

Submission is not to be used to avoid responsibility, nor as a coverup for weakness. A woman may try to make her husband live her life for her, make all her decisions and tell her what spiritual gifts to exercise. Then she will defend herself by saying, "I am just submitting." But she is not submitting. She is hiding.

Submission is not a sign of weakness. It is a sign of strength. A woman with a strong spirit and strong character can submit best, because she does not worry about the outcome. She does what is right before God and has great faith that He will take care of her regardless of circumstances or anything else. Her submission reveals her wisdom.[17]

Both men and women sometimes have the idea that submission means the woman has to do all the dirty work in the home. But remember the story in the Gospels of Jesus washing the disciples' feet?[18] Jesus was so certain of His identity, destiny and dignity that He had no problem stooping to minister to others in a menial way. His definitely was an act of humility!

We need to humble ourselves to serve others just as Christ did. But that is the two-way street, one where common courtesy prevails. Common courtesy seems to have been sacrificed in our day. What does it matter if, when you wash your clothes, you wash someone else's as well? What does it matter if you get someone else a glass of water when you are getting your own anyway? If we go out of our way to help others and minister to them, and do it as unto the Lord, we deserve His reward, not just our earthly rewards of gratitude from others.[19]

There is no inequality in the "Golden Rule." To show courtesy and care for others will be seen by God and, after all, we are to do all things that are pleasing to Him.[20]

And there is really no inequality in submission. When a wife chafes at the fact that she must submit decisions to her husband before she acts, she is forgetting that the same can be said of her husband. I am thankful for the story of Jacob in the Bible. Even after he heard directly from God to leave the land of his father-in-law, he submitted his decision to *both* his wives![21] Jacob probably would have chosen to follow God even if his wives were not in agreement; however, he had the common courtesy, and the godly initiative, to give them the opportunity to come into agreement with him.

Submission is a great tool for character building. God tests the faith of men and women as He calls them to submit themselves to His divine commands. Remember Abraham's willingness to sacrifice his son, Isaac, to God? That kind of submission is what led Abraham to greatness.

Submission precedes glorification. Proof of this principle is found in the Garden of Gethsemane, where Jesus' submission to the Father's will was so stressful to His human soul and body that "his sweat was like drops of blood."[22] But the submission of His will to His Father's led to His glorification and to God's will being done on earth.

Submission also takes courage! Sarah is one of only two women listed in the "Heroes of Faith" chapter of the book of Hebrews.[23] Why? She is listed because of her submission and great courage. Sarah, originally Sarai, was married to Abram, a man who lived an ordinary life in a pagan society. Then Abram began to see visions, to hear supernaturally from

Someone he said was the "true God," and he threw away the gods she had been raised to worship.

Then he asked her to call him by a new name, Abraham, and gave her a new name, Sarah. And he said the Lord promised them a child in their old age. Even when Sarah overheard the angel of the Lord speaking this, she laughed. Finally, however, she was able to believe with her husband. The result was that her faith took her through pregnancy and childbirth at almost a hundred years of age.[24] The conception was supernatural, but the delivery was natural. Talk about natural childbirth—that took courage!

Submission also requires faith. We elect government officials who enact laws that we will have to submit to later.[25] We may not realize it, but casting our votes for anyone is a show of faith on our part.

Having faith in God and trusting Him with your life enables you to entrust yourself to others. Submission is predicated on the understanding of God's transcendent glory, which is why we can truthfully say all things work together for the good of those called according to the purposes of God.[26]

Christ is our greatest example of submission. He, Who was God, submitted Himself to God. The Bible says that is why His prayers were so effective.[27] Jesus was so certain that God would take care of everything, and He submitted Himself so completely in faith to the Father's care, that He was able to entrust Himself even to men and walk willingly through the circumstances of His life.

We know Jesus submitted Himself to crucifixion by men even though He could have called "ten thousand angels." But He also allowed men their sins and errors throughout His life. For example, He gave the responsibility for the treasury to Judas even though He knew Judas would steal from it and eventually betray Him.

On the other hand, Jesus knew the times not to submit. Instead of submitting to the tradition of moneychangers in

the temple, He took swift action and cleaned them out.[28]
The time you stop submitting is at the point Jesus stopped
submitting—when submission would require an infringement
on your faith in God. You cannot submit indiscriminately.
However, it takes discernment to know when it is time to stop
submitting. Do not allow yourself to rationalize rebellion as a
justifiable decision not to submit.

Discernment brings great reward, but rebellion ends
in destruction.

If any authority asks you to do something not
consistent with the character of God, you have the right
and the obligation to refuse. Do not allow physical or
sexual abuse against yourself or others in your care under
a perverted sense of submission.

Another misunderstanding of submission is with wives
whose husbands are not serving God. Some women believe
they are not required to submit to unsaved husbands. But
the Bible says that by submission and the example of your
life, you may be able to lead them to the Lord.[29]

Jesus respected the religious authority of the Pharisees,[30]
even though He didn't agree with them. In fact, He knew
they were wrong and said they were "whited sepulchres."[31]
However, they were the religious authorities of their day, and
Jesus knew where to draw the line in submission.

There are times when leaders are wrong, so wrong
that even to know they are in authority grieves your spirit.
Yet, you can become equally wrong if you let it become a
root of bitterness or stir rebellion within you.[32] When you
disagree with authority in any form, you must be able to
commit it to God. Submit yourself to Him first, then tell
the leader what your disagreement is—in humility of spirit,
without emotional outbursts and without trying to control
the outcome. Your responsibility is to keep communication
lines open. The person in authority has the responsibility
to make the right decision.

When your "authority" is your husband and you desire
for him to change, you need to humble yourself before God

and become willing to change yourself. You must be as willing to change as you are desirous of him to change. But approaching any authority without prayer is folly. Just as Esther fasted and prayed three days, when you need to approach the authorities in your life, you need to do it *prayerfully*.

Submitting to the mistakes of others is difficult, but sometimes it is the only way that the other person will learn from God. A godly friend of ours learned this in a very practical way. Her husband came home from a Christian men's event changed, something she had been fervently asking God to bring about for years.

Then he began to discipline the children, which he had not done for years, and at which he was not as experienced as she, nor as adept. Also, he tried to make financial decisions, which turned out wrong because he did not have the broad picture she had from years of handling the checkbook.

At first, she corrected him. Those things were so simple to her, they had become second nature, so she was shocked by his errors. Then God convicted her of interference and lack of submission. She began submitting to his mistakes, and he began to learn from them and grow. Their marriage grew and prospered.

Soon he left his business to go into full-time ministry with her, and that is what they are doing today! What a great true story!

You develop trust in God as you submit to others.

You do not need a perfect leader if you have perfect trust in God.

CHAPTER FIVE

THE TRUTH ABOUT FORGIVENESS

NANCY

In order to submit, one must be able to forgive and forget past injuries or hurts. As odd as it may seem, one may need to learn to submit to love. Yes, love. Sometimes hurt and abused women submit more easily to rules and regulations than to the love and care of a man in an intimate relationship.

A letter we received illustrates this dilemma: "I have a problem that I have no solution for. My wife and I have been married about three years. Everything seems to be great except that she will not accept a compliment from me. Every time I try to encourage and build her up, she just shrugs her shoulders or tells me she does not believe me.

"Both of us were in marriages before where we were deeply hurt. My first wife left me for another man. I was devastated but promised myself that I would not make the same mistakes again. In this marriage, I am trying to do everything I know is right, but my wife won't accept it. It bothers me, because I'm afraid if she doesn't accept it from me, she'll go find another man from whom she will accept it. Please pray for me."

What a sad situation. This man's wife had been so hurt, she could not accept the love of a thoughtful husband who really needed her acceptance. Our prayer for her is to find healing through seeing God as He is—the loving and faithful Heavenly Father—so she can submit more and more to His awesome love and become the loving and receptive wife God and her husband want her to be.

What is your image of God? Do you see Him as an earthly father? Is your image of God clouded by man? There are Scriptures that warn against this.[1]

I learned this lesson in a dramatic way some years ago. Edwin and I were at one of those wonderful camp meetings where people could stay to do nothing but feast on the Word and find a quiet place to seek God. Having been a minister's wife for several years, I felt God had blessed my life in many ways and that I was a pretty well-adjusted Christian. But at the time, I was going through a trial which no one but God and my husband knew about. I had prayed many times about the situation but did not seem to get any answer from the Lord.

After Edwin taught one morning session, while he was ministering and talking to people, I slipped out of the meeting room and hastened to our cabin so I could have a time of prayer alone—just me and God. Now, I have not been given to seeing visions or to hearing audible utterances from God very often. However, that morning as I prayed, I got the distinct impression God was smiling at me. And He told me He was not hiding behind a newspaper. Until then, I never realized that I had attributed to my Heavenly Father a characteristic of my earthly father.

In a time of crisis, it seemed I was getting nowhere, but that was because I actually thought God was veiling His face from me. What a revelation I received. I had known it in my mind, but now I knew it in my heart: *God never hides from us!*[2]

In a short time, I was on the way to a solution when I discovered that *God is always there!* He will never leave us nor forsake us.[3] This promise is repeated throughout Scripture.

How do you see God?

Moses saw God in a burning bush; the Israelites saw Him as a cloud by day and a fire by night; Ezekiel saw God dazzling like fire; Daniel saw Him as the Ancient of Days; and Peter, James and John saw Christ transfigured as they gazed upon Him.[4]

There are many other places in the Bible where we see God in all His majesty and power. Never are we to see Him as a man because He is not.[5] He is the all-powerful, all-knowing, all-wise, majestic God, Ruler of the universe, Savior of our souls. He is great and mighty and will do for us above what we could even ask or think.[6] Learn to see Him as He really is, because God is love.[7]

When you submit to God's love, you are healed to love others and forgive past hurts, "forgetting those things which are behind," and reaching toward those things which are ahead.[8]

Edwin has a wonderful teaching on forgiveness—the key to leaving behind rejection, abuse, hurt and failures. Forgiveness is the key to breaking the cycle of sins passed from one generation to another. Forgiveness is the key to submitting to the love of your Heavenly Father and the love of those around you.

EDWIN

Christianity is not built on suppression or repression but on confession.

Confession of your own sins is essential to salvation. Confession of the sins of others is essential to forgiveness which is essential to true love.

Forgiveness is hard to extend naturally at times. That is why we need God to help us forgive as He forgives. Jesus Christ prayed the Father to send the Holy Spirit into our lives, and by His power, He has enabled us to forgive as

He does. When God forgives us, He never remembers our sins against us anymore. They are buried in "the depths of the sea."[9]

Jesus gave us a principle of the Kingdom about forgiveness that is simple yet incredibly profound. The depths of His truth cannot be exhausted but can be perceived by what He has done in the lives of others and what you can experience in your own life.

Let me give you the basic truth then the practical applications.

Before Jesus ascended into Heaven after His resurrection, He told the disciples, "Receive ye the Holy Ghost: Whosesoever sins ye remit, they are remitted unto them; and whosesoever sins ye retain, they are retained."[10]

The ecclesiastical authority for the absolution of sins in not an exclusive right of ministers, but it is the right of every believer to forgive sins by the power of Christ's Spirit in the same manner in which He forgave sins.

If we forgive sins, they are forgiven. If we do not forgive sins, they are kept. When you hold sins against someone, you actually are holding the sin within yourself. That hinders the effectiveness of your own prayers.[11] And, by holding that sin within you, you run the risk of doing the same thing yourself.

Jesus strictly admonished us that when we pray, we must forgive others.[12] In the "Lord's Prayer," He taught us to ask God to forgive us as we forgive others.[13] Forgiving others is not optional. In choosing to forgive, we choose to obey or rebel.

Forgiving as God forgives must be done by the power of His Spirit, which is the reason Jesus prefaced His command to forgive with a charge to be filled with the Holy Spirit. Only the Spirit of God can enable us to forgive divinely.

After an early church service one Sunday, a woman told me why she needed to forgive. Plump and in her thirties, she looked like a grown-up church girl who had never missed a week in Sunday School.

"Two years ago, my husband left me for another woman and took my children," she said. "I got a job and moved to an apartment building near my workplace. Six months ago, I came home late from shopping and got into the apartment complex elevator. Suddenly, a man jumped in after me, put a knife to my throat and raped me. It was horrible!

"I was anguished, angry, and I blamed God for it. I felt He should have protected me but had not. Deep resentment toward Him formed almost overnight. I got back at Him by refusing to go to church. I was so lonely, confused and hurt, I did not know what to do.

"Then I realized I needed to forgive God. Of course, I know God does not need to be forgiven, because He is God. But when I heard the principle about 'release,' I knew I needed to forgive God for myself, to get freedom from all I was feeling and thinking."

This woman apparently had believed that being a Christian meant living a "charmed life" where nothing could go wrong. When things did go wrong, she blamed God. When she finally realized it was not God Who caused all her problems, but that God was the only One Who could help her, the revelation changed her life.

In Atlanta one day, I heard another story from a sharp, sophisticated young lady who just oozed with personality. Finally, she had learned to be free from guilt but wanted to confess it to someone out loud. I was the "someone" she chose.

Somewhat nervously she said, "I feel I have to tell you this to get it out of my life. When my parents were having problems, my mother moved out and another woman moved in. It was a bad scene for a while until it all got straightened out. Anyhow, during that time when things were all fouled up, my brother and I got fouled up, too. It was just during that one period of time, but it has stayed with me for years like a heaviness on my mind and a hard place in my heart.

"Then the truth about forgiveness hit me, and I realized I could be free from that weight. I did what the

Bible says, forgave, and it felt as if a ten-ton truck was lifted off me. It does not bother me at all anymore!"

In Dallas once-after I ministered, a mother hung around the door until the crowd died down, then approached me. Her words came out in a rush, like a cascading waterfall.

"My daughter had been living with a man for three years. I didn't approve of it at all. I resented him living with my daughter without any prospect of marriage. It was affecting my relationship with her and making life hard on the whole family.

"Then, I prayed the prayer of release. I needed to get rid of my hard feelings toward both of them. When I prayed the prayer, I forgave the man for everything he had ever done, starting with being born. But it was from my heart. I meant it. Everything he had done, I forgave him.

"Do you know what? Just three weeks later, he proposed marriage to my daughter. Now, they are getting married, and I actually like my son-in-law!"

When the torrent of words ended, she clapped her hands, laughed ecstatically and, as abruptly as she started, walked away.

Then there was the single woman who was jilted and became cynical about men. She was lonely and desired companionship, but her attitude pushed men away and encased her in a shell. With time, her attitude degenerated almost into hatred, but she was "saved" by the prayer of release.

Through Jesus Christ, forgiveness for all sins of all men has been secured eternally. However, it must be asked for and received. It is a free gift, an act of love. *Forgiveness is the essence of mercy; mercy is the essence of grace; grace is the essence of love; and love is the essence of holiness.*

True holiness is manifested in real forgiveness. Some religious people profess to be holy yet hold unforgiveness toward the irreligious and, by doing so, prove they are not wholly holy.

Outward accoutrements of holy living mean little to God if the heart is not adorned with forgiveness.

Forgiveness is never earned. It is always a gift by grace from the love of God shed abroad in our hearts by the Holy Spirit. When you forgive as God forgives, you may remember what happened but never remember it against anyone again. There is freedom from the hurt and pain of the experience. Then it becomes possible for God's transcendent glory to turn it around and make it all work for good.

I remember words from a Presbyterian pastor that brought a glow to my heart. Alone in my hotel room, with the phone cradled against my shoulder and my feet on the table, I leaned back across the divan to listen to his story.

"You can't believe how much good has been done from that truth about forgiveness," he said. "When my daughter divorced, it was tough on me. I felt like I suffered a lot from it because of my status and position in the church and community.

"As a result of my feelings, I made the situation hard on her. Doing that, I realize now, seemed to appease my pride. When your message of 'release' hit me, I admitted my response to her situation had been based entirely on how it reflected on me, not how it affected her. All of a sudden, it occurred to me that I was not ministering to my own daughter in her hour of crisis. If it had been someone else, I would have given comfort and godly counsel. But it was my own daughter, and I did not minister to her!

"First, I asked God to forgive me. Then I asked her to forgive me of my pride and prejudice. We had a beautiful time of reconciliation. Now I am able to minister to my daughter and her former husband. With the way they are responding, I am thinking perhaps I can help them get back together!"

This was a prophetic fulfillment. God said through the Prophet Malachi that the Lord would "turn the heart of the fathers to the children, and the heart of the children to their fathers, lest I come and smite the earth with a curse."[14]

Are you holding something against someone? Do you need to forgive yourself? Others? God? You can receive the Holy Spirit to enable you to pray right now. By forgiveness, you release; by unforgiveness, you retain.

You can be released and release others by the ability of God's Spirit through the authority of His Word now. Pray this prayer:

> Father, I come to You now, in the Name of Jesus. By faith, I ask You to forgive and cleanse me of all my sins. You said unless I forgive, You would not forgive me. So right now, I ask You to forgive me and cleanse my heart and mind of all sin.
>
> By faith, I receive the power of the Holy Spirit into my life. By the ability of Your Spirit and the authority of Your Word, I forgive that person who has sinned against me. I release his sin out of my life.
>
> Thank You, Lord, for what You are doing to make me free from my own sin and the sins of others.

Pray that prayer in your own words, in your own way, and allow the Holy Spirit to make you free. You know you are free when you can remember what happened but not hold it against anyone anymore.

Be free.

Live free.

NANCY

And when you forgive, *let go!* Discipline yourself to capture every painful, angry thought and submit it to the Lord. A dear friend of ours has kept her family in an uproar for several years now. Her husband had an adulterous affair, but he repented and submitted himself to the leadership of the church for restoration, recommitting himself to her. However, she still brings up the past, both jokingly and in anger.

By contrast, read this letter from a woman who had enough pain to fuel bitterness for a lifetime but chose not to:

"My mother was deserted by her alcoholic parents and left with an aunt who did not want her. She became pregnant with me to get out of that house, but another girl got pregnant by my father at the same time. So Mom supported me by becoming a prostitute.

"When I was four, she married a man who later adopted me. They both worked, so I grew up a lonely latchkey kid. They had high expectations for me and called me names when I failed at dance, modeling, piano and everything they tried to do for me. I also failed socially, being very shy and having no close friends.

"Evidently, I was pretty, which made them worry about what would happen to me, so they told me I was plain and ugly. They were strict, not allowing me to go outside, talk to or about boys, and called me boy crazy when I began to wear makeup.

"At thirteen, I was raped. I never told them because I thought they would blame me. The boy told everyone, however, and I got a reputation for being cheap. I just wanted to be loved and accepted, but I felt ugly, rejected, unwanted, dirty and cheap. I wanted to die.

"I began to live up to the reputation the boy gave me. When I thought a guy really cared about me, which he usually didn't, I would give in and have sex. I guess I felt that kind of love was better than none at all. At sixteen, I married a man who I thought was the one because he hung around even after having sex. My life with him was miserable. He drank, took drugs and brought his girlfriends into our home even with me there. He encouraged me to have other affairs, which I did, hoping to hurt him. I felt I couldn't leave him because it would shame my parents and just leave me at the mercy of other men who would use me.

"When I was 22, I could not even remember how many men I had slept with. I saw a psychiatrist, who hospitalized me for two weeks for severe depression. When I left the hospital, I never went back to my husband. Instead, I decided to get revenge by using men the way they had used me—funny, but I still felt I was the one being used.

"I moved in with my present husband before I was divorced from the first, and we had two children. Still unhappy, I finally called out to God in my despair. My husband and I were both saved. He gave up drugs, I started losing weight; we both felt good. We worked on our marriage, and the Lord gloriously healed it—except I still had a hard time fully giving myself to him.

"I knew I had forgiven myself and my first husband, but until I heard you minister about retaining sins through unforgiveness, I didn't realize that I hadn't forgiven my parents. My mom didn't trust me because of her promiscuity, and because she retained that sin, I ended up being promiscuous also. My mom was not wanted, and because she did not forgive her parents, she made me feel burdensome and unwanted.

"Their sins were passed on to my children through me. My parents were critical, and I have ended up being critical with my children. There is a lot more, but *the cycle has been broken!* I forgive my parents, my husband, myself and every man who ever hurt me. I release all the guilt, anger, hate, shame, fear and pain through the power of God and count it against them—and me—no more! I feel beautiful, clean and free to be a wonderful wife to my husband. *I am a new woman, washed clean!*"

God is so wonderful to care so much for us! This young woman had truly learned to forgive and let go of the past. Here is another letter, written by a woman who is now in the process of leading her entire family to the Lord:

"For many years, I was physically abused by my father and grandfathers. Many times, from the age of nine, I attempted suicide. My father, an alcoholic and adulterer, made it clear to me that women are no good. My continuous search for love brought me into a sexually promiscuous life.

My trust in men was limited, and I had bouts with alcohol, mental breakdowns and physical illnesses. But God is remaking me. Now I see the world more and more through the eyes of the Lord."

You may not have had an experience like these women, or perhaps, your own experience was worse. Whichever, things of the past tend to gnaw at women unless they forgive and release them.

As Edwin said, release all of that and be free! Experience the depth of God's love in your life. This healthiness of spirit, freedom of thought, peace of heart and righteousness of attitude can be yours today.

CHAPTER SIX

THE POWER OF SEX

NANCY

Sex is not a subject I launch into without any hesitation but is something extremely private and personal to me. However, from reading the last chapter, you can see how much our lives are affected by sexuality—our own and others'. We are bombarded daily with messages about sex and sexiness. Whether married or single, we simply must face the issue and deal with it in a realistic way.

It is only fair to let you know that my perspective is from forty-plus years of monogamous marriage. Over those years, Edwin and I have not only built a good sexual relationship, but an entire life of intimacy and oneness. The longer we are married, the more integrated our lives become in every aspect.

Over the past decade or more, I have read and assessed many books for or about women which were written to help them in the bedroom, especially to liberate them from old stereotypical attitudes that sex was somehow dirty. The enlightenment in some of these books is good, because sex is meant for our good, for pleasure and to make reproduction a thrill for us to experience.

There comes a point, however, in both print and visual media, where I draw the line. Sensational, glamorized scenes showing or describing a couple in intimate relations are often not only embarrassing, but ridiculous to the point of being laughable. Yet there are people who will copy the actors, thinking they will find the same intimacy that was portrayed. People then commit fornication or adultery and are deceived into thinking they are building a relationship.

The truth is that sex is an *expression* of intimacy, not a *means* to intimacy. Sex certainly is not a means to hold a relationship together.

It is difficult for me to understand the shallowness, the crassness and the utter cynicism that some people must have in order to treat sex as casually and carnally as they do. They engage in sex as if it had no effect on them, on God, the rest of the world or their partner. However, everyone's sin affects everyone else. That is evident by the sexual permissiveness in the world today. One person's sin infects another, and it grows until everyone's sin jointly taints the entire world. Legislators find it difficult to rule against something of which they themselves are guilty. The result is that sexual acts are legal today which a generation ago were taboo even to mention.

One of the reasons people accept this is because they assume the Church has nothing to offer on the subject. Contrary to the beliefs of many, God does have something to say, and His guidelines for sex do not promote poor, inhibited sexual relationships! God's guidelines and commands actually ensure a great sex life, one that is pure and guilt-free, increasing in both emotional and physical satisfaction as the years go by.

A little "self-test" I heard of years ago may help you discover your own underlying attitudes toward sex. Can you read "Song of Solomon" without embarrassment, taking it as the whole Word of God? Can you realize not only the sensuality of the book, but also the freedom to love that God portrays?

Freedom to love with the full expression of your sexuality is what God intends for the marriage relationship. We can learn to live up to God's Word even in our sex lives! That takes prayer, forgiveness, confession of sin and a purifying of the mind to accomplish. Unforgiveness and bitterness can actually hinder sexual fulfillment. This is all the more reason to seek after righteousness and not engage in sex outside of marriage.

The wretched sex lives that some people lead are not the result of God imposing Himself on man. They are the result of not following the Lord's commands. The problems with sex today are not due to the restraint of the Church but to the permissiveness of the world. This reminds me of Ahab who accused Elijah of being the one who was troubling Israel, when it was Ahab's sins that had brought trouble to the country. Elijah was simply trying to restore the country through obedience to God.[1] Only after the outbreak of AIDS are people considering what the Church has known all along. The answer to good, healthy sex is abstinence before marriage and fidelity after. Anything other than that opens the door to all sorts of problems.

After Edwin began to bring messages along this line, it seemed that half our mail started to come from Christians who were battling, or had recently overcome, some kind of sex-related problem. It is a shame that the world has imposed itself so much on the Church that saints, saved by the blood of Jesus, are still having such a struggle in an area that is meant to be one of God's greatest blessings to mankind. The marriage relationship is intended to be an earthly example of the relationship between Christ and the Church.[2] When so many Christian marriages have difficulties, how distorted our perception must be of Christ's love for us!

Thousands upon thousands of Christians are struggling with problems related to sex. Some choose to believe the scintillating sex lives portrayed by the media, but others look to the Word of God, which is the true answer to their needs.

The following letter is from a woman desiring God's best in a very distressing situation:

"I need your help. In brief, this is my second marriage and his first. I met Kevin four years after I became a Christian. When we dated, he was very aggressive and lustful, and, at first, I yielded. Then God gave me the strength to say "no." After we married, I learned he had been abused by his mother. He says he has forgiven her, yet it is as though all his affectionate desires are blocked.

"All I know is that from the day we were married until today, six and a half years later, he has not desired a physical relationship. And, until he heard your ministry, he masturbated many times each day. At first, he was in total denial that anything was wrong. Now he is aware, but we are still at a stalemate physically. Yes, we have had the marriage act and without difficulty but with a span of nine months in between. It has only been when I finally confront him that he will even try. I feel like a total nag and don't understand him. I have cried out to God continually, and I know some steps have been taken. I guess I am just asking for some staying power and prayer until this marriage is totally healed."

That is a pathetic state for a Christian marriage. Along with blocking natural affection and desires, this man has also blocked a lot of hostility, hurt and anger. He needs to release his mother's sins out of his life, and then together, he and his wife can work toward intimacy.

As Edwin says, "Prayer produces intimacy." When you have a problem with sex, consistent times of prayer together will work wonders as nothing else will.

A 26-year-old wife wrote about a more common problem:

"I don't enjoy oral sex and my husband knows it, but I do it because he wants it. It seems like he is not satisfied with 'regular sex' anymore. But when oral sex is involved in our lovemaking, he doesn't even know where I'm at—he just becomes a big sponge. He says that it makes him feel loved, and that if he doesn't have it, he is tempted with pornography.

"Shouldn't he be the one to resist? If he gives in and buys a magazine, is it my fault? Why is oral sex wrong? Is it just the selfishness of it? How does the biblical principle that our bodies are not our own but our mate's apply to this?"

She sounded like such a lovely young lady, so desirous to do God's will if only she knew what He wanted her to do. There are many, many scriptures about purity, holiness and the "clean" and "unclean" in the Bible. I did not address them all but answered her in a way that I hope will help any other woman who finds herself in a similar quandary. I wrote:

"We are receiving many letters about oral sex. I want to give you as balanced a reply as I can according to what I have heard and read, both in the Bible and through Christian teachers.

"I find that some Christian leaders condemn it vigorously, and at the other extreme, some advocate it completely. Many ministers fall in between, saying they do not see anything in the Bible against it; however, they personally do not practice it. Concerning sexual practices, only bestiality and masochism are forbidden specifically, they say. However, some believe that Romans 14 applies to many situations not specifically dealt with in the Bible.

"May I give you as objective a view as I possibly can? Firstly, the Bible makes no reference to oral sex. The Old Testament in Leviticus 20:18 gives instruction not to engage in sexual intercourse during a woman's menstrual cycle. Only the Song of Solomon gives us any idea of God's view of sexual love. Why is this book in the Bible? Because in it, God shows us a very beautiful but voluptuous and sensual pattern of loving for a husband and wife, modeled after the beautiful love relationship between Christ and the Church.

"In the New Testament, there are clues to sex in marriage found in Hebrews 13:4, where it states that the marriage bed is undefiled. Besides this reference, we have Romans 14:14, which states that 'there is nothing unclean of itself,' and

Ephesians 5:24-33, which talks about wives' submission to husbands and husbands' great responsibility to love their wives as themselves and as Christ loves the Church.

"I think the key to your dissatisfaction is revealed in your letter when you say that in the act of oral sex, your husband does not even know where you are. Farther on in your letter, you state that there is a selfishness involved. Certainly, it is true that if your husband is not providing for your pleasure in the marriage bed as a couple, you will never achieve the sexual intimacy that God desires you to have.

"As many Christian writers on this subject emphasize, each partner always needs to be very conscious of what gives the other the most pleasure and to be looking out for the feelings and needs of each other. Without this giving, at the expense of self sometimes, a couple will never attain true sexual intimacy.

"I do hope you will get some counseling on this matter and check your local Christian bookstore for recent books on this subject by Christian authors. Perhaps you and your husband could read such a book together, a few passages a day followed by Bible reading and prayer. God bless you. God wants you to be happy and fulfilled, and He will give you the desires of your heart as you seek Him and His will for your life."

Let me encourage you, single and married alike—no matter what situation or difficulty you now find yourself in, give your sexuality over to God. Let Him create in you what He originally intended you to have. Allow Him to purify your heart, emotions, thoughts and motivation for sex. Use your sexuality wisely, carefully and with a great deal of respect for God and your husband, if you have one. Then, in marriage, enjoy!

EDWIN

A pastor's wife sat talking to me in her office one day. She was realistically appraising our ministry to men, commending us and commenting on the necessity for such a ministry today. Then she told me as a matter of fact that I had a problem with women! Instantly intrigued, I listened carefully to her story.

"We had a couple of young men who were converted in this church," she explained. "They were weight lifters, you know, body builders. We jokingly referred to them as 'Holy Hunks.' The problem was the women wouldn't leave them alone. The young men were astonished at how sexually available and seductive these so-called Christian women were.

"Ed," she concluded, "what you are doing with the men is great, but some of the women will undermine everything you are doing if you don't teach them as well. So, teach them!"

This gracious pastor's wife certainly did not intend to impugn women in general, but she had a valid point. A woman holds the power of sex, and the extent of that power is awesome. But what women need to realize is that sex is sacred to God.

God is a God of covenants. For every covenant, there is an external "sign" of the covenant. In the covenant between God and Abraham, the sign was circumcision.[3] In the New Covenant God has made with believers in His Son, Jesus Christ, the believers' hearts are "circumcised," and the external sign is water baptism and communion.[4]

Marriage is a covenant relationship; therefore, there must be a sign.

Sex is the sign of the covenant of marriage.

God's Word says that "marriage is honourable in all, and the bed undefiled."[5] That statement is not a license for lust. It does not mean that "anything goes" in the bedroom such as unbridled lust, "kinky sex" or sadistic satisfaction.

Sex is the highest physical union between a man and woman and is to reflect their union in spirit. Sex is a celebration of the marriage covenant and is to be entered into with an expression of love.

Sex was not made for lusting and getting but for loving and giving.

Lust limits; love releases.

Lust is insatiable; love is easily satisfied.

The Creator of sex was God, not the devil. Anything God creates, He makes good.[6] God made sex good; sin makes it bad.

God gave woman the power of sex as part of her "uniqueness." He did not give its power to the man but to the woman. She has it; he wants it. If she doesn't give it, he won't get it.

To take sexual satisfaction from a woman without her voluntary submission is a rapacious assault and is a criminal act. Rape, incest, molestation are all sins against a woman and *always* need to be considered a criminal act in a system of jurisprudence.

God created woman as a "helpmeet" for man, to complete him. The man originally was given dominion over the earth, with the command from God to oversee the reproductive process of all that was in the Garden of Eden.[7] The woman was created and given the power of sex to "help meet" the needs of the man personally and as he exercised his God-given stewardship over the earth.

Woman was created to be the "completer," not a "competitor." When a woman uses the power of sex to seduce a man, she becomes the competition of God in his life. He must choose her or God. Seducing him into choosing her puts him at enmity with God through sinning against God.

When a wife shows love, ministers to and cares for her husband using her power of sex, she nurtures the marriage, and by fulfilling him, encourages her husband to press on in whatever his outside endeavors may be.

Society has created the images of "good" and "bad" women. "Good" women take care of the home, have children and oversee the household economy. "Bad" women enjoy sex.

More than once the media has portrayed the prostitute with the "heart of gold" as heroine to the hero while the "good" woman stands by stupidly and watches the excitement. How asinine. The truth is "good" women enjoy sex, too! They enjoy it as much as men, desire it as much as men, are often better at it than men.

Christian women need to understand that sex is "okay" for good women! They must realize that sex is sacred. God did not make sex something "dirty," something to hide. When entered into in a loving covenant relationship, it is a gift from God, praiseworthy and holy.

Sex is not an athletic contest where people "score" in competition. Nor is the bed to be a battlefield or a foil for blackmail. Many a woman will blackmail a man by withholding her sexual favor until he complies with her wishes, demands or desires. They abuse their power of sex and are wrong in what they do.

The desire for sex differs, as does the style, frequency, inhibitions, fears and images. An appetite for sex can be more imagined than real. In counseling an irreligious couple who professed "sexual freedom," I discovered the real truth was that they had sex once a month, and their "freedom" was a farce.

One young Christian woman questioned her sanity because of the amount of time she spent thinking about sex. When she went to her pastor, he found that she and her husband might wait as long as six months between incidents of intimacy. When they changed to twice a week based on his counsel, she discovered sanity was not the issue.

Jane's case went even further. She was middle-aged by the time she divorced her husband. He had a nervous breakdown, was irritable, unstable and constantly needed help to battle his "sin." After their divorce, a counselor discovered that Jane thought sex was "dirty." She felt guilty after engaging in intercourse, and the most she and her husband made love was twice a year. She had accused him that his wanting and thinking about sex so much was a "sin." When asked why she thought this way, it finally came to light that this was what her mother had taught her as a girl to protect her from premarital promiscuity. How tragic, stupid and unnecessary!

Educating the young concerning sex is the responsibility of the Church.

God made sex. Yet to this day, the Church has abrogated its effort in this regard, allowing the world to pollute, contaminate and corrupt the minds and lives of young men and women who sincerely want to do right. We *are* our brother's keeper. We are keepers of his understanding by teaching God's truths, enabling him to live righteously. People perish for lack of knowledge.[8]

Teaching children that sex is "bad" is as bad as giving them condoms to engage in "safe sex." Condoms are not the answer to herpes or AIDS—virginity is. Children need to know sex is sacred and that any sex outside the marriage covenant is defiled. Only in marriage is it undefiled. Adultery, fornication, lesbianism and homosexuality are all engaged in outside the marriage covenant and therefore are defiled. Such things are sin. Sin causes broken marriages, lives, heartache, disease and even death.

Children are often the victims. A basic sociological fact is that children need parents who are sexually committed to each other, parents who enjoy a stable relationship. Parents who "swing" are not simply unstable, they are lethal.

Ultimately, it is the Church that holds the "ideal" for marriage and family. The "ideal" is virginity until marriage and fidelity after. However, this is not the "real life" of secular society. Immorality seems to be more prevalent than morality.

Even the Church is suffering from infidelity among its members. Premarital sex is not the exclusive domain of the irreligious. Single men and women professing Christ engage in sexual immorality.[9] Because the sentence against an evil work is not executed speedily, there is no restraint in them from doing evil.[10] They do not understand that sex is sacred, and therefore, by their lasciviousness, they profane the Name of God.

Simply because some church leader has been discovered to have engaged in illicit practices is no excuse for others to do the same. *Excuses are not reasons.* The atrocity of a church leader's sex sin does not lie in the sin itself, but in the fact that when the sin is exposed for the world to see, it allows those who deny the claims of Christ to blaspheme our Lord.[11] The blasphemy of the worthy Name by which we are saved is the greatest wickedness.

In attempting to forestall promiscuity, most preachers stress the negative results of promiscuity, not the godly principles of moral purity. In two of my books— *Communicating, Sex and Money*[12] and *Sexual Integrity*[13]—I discuss why men and women need to be virgins at the time of marriage. There is a positive aspect to sexual purity to be taught.

Sex within marriage is often difficult even without all the errors and misconceptions that some drag into their relationship. In marriage, the more dominant a man is, the more he is defeated in the bedroom. When a woman does not have veto power over a man's actions anywhere but in the bedroom, that is where she will exercise it. Unless he violates her rapaciously, the bedroom is where she knows she can win.

On the other hand, a woman's sexual "put-downs" and unwillingness demean a man's prowess. His ability to engage in sex is rooted deeply in his desire for that reproductive process and is inextricably incorporated in his ego.

I will never forget the comment made by a close minister friend, as we discussed the unfortunate prevalence of pornography and man's predilection for it.

He said, "I am convinced that one of the major reasons men are attracted to pornography is that the men are always able, and the women are always willing."

Pornography popularized oral sex which, as Nancy explained, has created such a problem in some marriages today. Pornography and romantic novels created the myth that every sexual encounter needs to climax with mutual orgasm. Not true. Actually, trying to achieve that every time is a hindrance. When it does not occur, each wonders, "Whose fault is it...?"

Mutual orgasm may be the epitome, where each partner can express gratitude, but it is not the norm, nor need it be. A genuinely loving man is just as gratified to satisfy his wife without thought of his own satisfaction. That is the giving in loving. Why should a woman be constantly pressured to satisfy her husband's needs while hers go unmet? When such is the case, and he is unwilling to change, there are other considerations that we will deal with in a later chapter.

Then there are the women with unsaved husbands who know nothing of the covenant relationship into which they have entered. In Florida several years ago, I was invited to speak to a friend's congregation on a Sunday evening. After ministering on the subject of "the sacredness of sex," I commented to the pastor that I hoped no one had been offended.

"No," he answered quickly. "I tell the women who have unsaved husbands and attend here regularly to be sure to go home Sunday evenings and love their husbands. If they go home with a holier-than-thou attitude, with a don't-touch-me piety, the husband will be jealous of the church and resent the pastor. Someone offended is harder to win than a strong city, the Bible says,[14] and a woman who acts like that will have a difficult time convincing an offended husband that both she and God love him."

His comments took me by surprise, but they showed wisdom. By loving and making love, a wife not only shows her desire for her husband, but because of her warm and loving response after church, her husband will appreciate what attending church does for her. It can change his attitude toward God and the church.

Enjoyable sex gives rise to the joy of the Lord. God's praiseworthiness is as real in the sanctuary of the home as that of the church. It is equally as righteous to express gratitude and praise to God in the bedroom for the covenant of marriage as it is in church for the covenant of salvation.

If you are married, learn to enjoy what God has provided. If you are not, the next chapter will help you wait.

CHAPTER SEVEN

MYTHS OF MARRIAGE

EDWIN

"And they lived happily ever after."

With that closing line from a fictional novel, a myth of marriage is created.

Nancy and I have lived together for far more years than we each lived alone. Although we have experienced genuine happiness in those years, the element that has made our marriage good is the joy of the Lord. "All true joy is born out of sorrow" is the principle our Lord gives us.[1] Sorrow, not happiness, is life's greatest teacher.[2] The evidence of this principle is found even in salvation; you will never know the joy of salvation until you experience the sorrow of repentance for sin.

The troubled times Nancy and I have gone through are the slabs of mortar that seal together the bricks of happiness. Bonded collectively, these elements have built a true and lasting joy in our marriage.

When you think of building your marriage, take a good look at the raw materials and at the person with whom you will be sharing them. The decision to marry is the second most important decision anyone will ever make. The first is to believe on Jesus Christ as Lord and Savior.

The Bible says, "A good name is rather to be chosen than great riches."[3] The man you marry is within your power of choice right up to the moment you say the wedding vows. While you have the power of choice, go for the man with the "good name," the man with character. It takes discernment to look past the personality to see the real man.

A single woman of good Christian character needs to be all the more careful. Her sweetness of spirit, kindness and gentleness make her the most attractive woman in the world. "As you begin to seek God, men will begin to seek you," is the way humorist Van Crouch puts it. Funny, but true.

New construction is always easier than reconstruction. It is not wise to enter a marriage, live through hurts and disappointments, then have to rebuild the marriage to make it last. Go for character now. All the other externals and circumstances are changeable.

Over the years of my marriage to Nancy, the world has changed, even as we have. Fluctuations in society necessitate alterations in living. *The only constant in maturity is change.* Today, women must face issues that cast relationships in a different light and require adjustments in lifestyle. Truth does not vary, but the way truth is applied in our lives can change. Therefore, expectations must change.

When I was a boy growing up in the Los Angeles area, the purpose of schools was to give children information that was not readily available or accessible in the home. Books, learned teachers and disciplines were provided for my education. That was the purpose of schools from their inception. Only decades ago, information concerning the world was scarce. Current information took days, weeks or months to reach people around the world.

My first job as a very young man was standing on a street corner selling newspapers. I sold the news of the day to drivers passing by, dodging traffic while I tried to sell as many papers as I could. Little did I realize that the very accessibility to such news would eventually change the world and require changes in the way I lived in the future.

Now we live in a day of "information saturation." However, the difference between yesterday's information and that of today is that most of the information today is trivia. The pursuit of trivia is more than a game, it is a way of life. Television's in-depth programming is relegated to little-seen networks or stations, while the powerful networks provide "fluff and stuff." Newspapers headline the news, as does television, and the full content or substance of the news is never known.

Politicians get their exposure on television in "bites." Modern man deals with "images" rather than "issues."

This is "the age of trivialization."

Yet life itself is far from trivial, and the issues confronting women are real. Working women are no longer an anomaly but a normality in society.

An article in *Savvy Woman* magazine[4] reported the statistics that in America in 1987, 61 percent of married women worked. The prediction is that by 1990, it will be 65 percent. By the year 2000, it will be 75 percent. No wonder child care has become a major issue in America.

Women average about 70 percent of the salary that men earn, but it is expected to rise to 90 percent.

In 1957, 80 percent of the people polled said those who did not want to marry were abnormal, sick, neurotic or immoral. However, in 1983, only 25 percent of the people polled were negative toward the unmarried—a vast shift in societal perception.

Changes in work habits force changes in home life. In 1987, only 15 percent of meals at home were cooked in conventional ovens. Microwave cooking became the normal way of life with pre-prepared meals beginning to replace conventional canned goods or fresh goods.

Women have 25 percent less leisure time than men, and women with children under 12 have 31 percent less.

No wonder the idea of husbands sharing the housework has become a major issue.

The ideas of morality also have undergone a massive change. In 1986, by the age of 17, most young people had had sex. In 1987, it was estimated that 80 percent of all boys, and 60 percent of all girls had engaged in some degree of sexual activity by the age of 19, according to the same survey.

The expectation some women have that they will live in the same manner as their mothers or grandmothers can be a presumption—a myth. The world simply is different.

Life is where you find it and what you make of it. Living cannot be ignored, abandoned, escaped or denied. Preaching a Christian message and requiring godliness in the same pastoral setting as at the time of Christ, and expecting people to relate to the same environment Jesus lived in, is foolishness.

However, the principles Jesus gave us for living are as real, modern, useful, basic and eternal as in the days He walked the earth and revealed them to us. "Jesus Christ [is] the same yesterday, and today, and for ever,"[5] but the world is not.

The "Proverbs 31 woman" today is no different from the one in Bible days. In fact, her responsibilities have expanded, the stress may be greater, an ability to manage more necessary and her time more precious. Time management in industrialized nations is not something for large corporations only but for the running of a household.

Blessed is the woman whose husband provides a livelihood that does not require her to work. Yet today's woman without outside work still involves herself in charitable activities, community enterprises and pleasure pursuits and, in doing so, keeps the pressure on.

Economic changes have brought competitiveness between men and women into sharp focus. This competitiveness carries over into the home and even the church. Women demand equality in church government as well as in civil government. The changes and resulting tension cannot be ignored.

The greatest danger for a single woman in contemplating marriage is "mythical mating" or "magical thinking." To marry with the idea that she will live some kind of charmed, carefree life is to entertain a myth. Another myth is in trying to convince herself that what she sees in a prospective spouse is not real. That is deception, pure and simple.

Marrying someone because he is sexy, fun to be with, feels safe or is a "great guy" is not just unwise—it is stupid. "Mythical mating" is fictitious reasoning. Creating something out of nothing is a form of magical thinking. God is a miracle worker, not a magician.

Facing reality is the only way to live. *Truth and reality are synonymous.* Jesus is the ultimate reality because He is Truth. To marry, or stay married, you need the Spirit of Jesus Christ to lead and guide you into "all truth."[6]

Recently, I went to breakfast with a gentleman who had suffered a fall from the heights of national religious acclaim. Now he was sitting in a coffee shop with a friend, talking about the future of his life and ministry and about his wife, Beth. He said he did not know if their marriage would survive because of what he had gone through. I braced him with the truth that the problem was not what he had gone through but the condition of his life now.

I told him, "You have never given yourself to anyone, although Beth has loved you, trusted you, stood with you and given herself to you. Your ministry was based on what you learned, not on what you believed. Beth has found a job and is making a new life for herself based on what she can produce, not on your promises. She is facing reality about herself, you and her future. You are still trying to escape without having to face reality, repent and make restitution."

Beth had been at the top, the pinnacle, the apex of fame and fortune with him, but she could never make him see that it was based on ephemeral substance and not concrete reality. She hoped against hope that the bubble would never burst. She hid from the reality of his duplicities. She covered over the facts for fear of facing them. Finally, it all came apart.

In ministering to them both, I talked with Beth a few days later on the telephone. When he is home, she no longer pretends things are not as they seem. Instead, she is rebuilding her life based on the truth of her relationship with the Lord and her personal ability. It has not been easy for her, but today she is more secure in the Lord and in herself, more functional and able to perform with a greater degree of excellence than ever before. She is enjoying success and living.

Beth cannot go back and relive those years, but she would give you a word of warning: "Face the realities early on. Don't wait until you are forced to face them."

When a woman marries, she marries the character of the man, not his personality. *Whatever a man is before marriage, he will be more of after marriage.*

The single life can be difficult, but it is far easier than what Beth and others like her have suffered. Consider this letter written to me by a single Christian woman in Malaysia:

"Thank you on behalf of us ladies for speaking out boldly to men who live far below the image that God has made them to be. Some women choose marriage. Others opt for singlehood because of what they see or because they refuse to settle for second best. They want the best God can provide. But how do we relate carefully and meaningfully between singles of different sexes?

"I wonder if you will agree with me that too many times it is the ladies who take the initiative and do what the men actually should do in courtship. Perhaps for fear of rejection, nothing is said between singles, so one, whether male or female, doesn't even know when a relationship or commitment begins and when it ends. Everything is left dangling. Some become hurt, confused, hardened and/or bitter and thus close themselves to future relationships."

Her letter speaks for single women everywhere. The truth is that God is doing a work in men today, making them more responsible, taking them from the "era of the mediocre man" into a period of true manhood which is Christlikeness.

But the issue for women is in how they perceive a man. A rogue is not a knight in tarnished armor. Yet the most unlikely man, provided he has a heart for God, may end up a spiritual giant. The poorest urchin can become a "king." Your evidence is in whether or not God tells you to marry him. This is something about which Nancy has more to say.

NANCY

Some women seem to want to hang on to myths instead of letting go, facing reality and accepting what God has for their lives. Here are five other common myths about marriage.

Myth #1: I have some misgivings, but it will all work out.

I have met more than one woman whose life was wrecked because of this myth. Joyce is one who stands out in my mind. She did not have the peace of God[7] when she married. She knew there is a God-given peace when you are operating in His will, but she rationalized away her doubts and married this man in the midst of a confused crisis.

He abused her, humiliated her, never held a job and molested their daughter, who is disturbed to this day. He made Joyce's life a hell instead of the heaven God intended her to have. When he finally left, she began getting her life back in order, but she suffers guilt every time she looks at their daughter, the unwitting victim of her poor decision.

The myth that you should go against your better judgment, hoping things will work out, is a false optimism and a lie of the devil! If a woman is not absolutely sure God has brought her and this man together, she needs to tell him, "Goodbye. I am so sorry, but you are not the one God wants me to marry."

Generally, this will result in a sense of relief. Prayer, soul-searching and a godly counselor such as your pastor will help you uncover why you thought you needed that particular man in the first place.

Myth #2: I can change him after we are married.

Nothing could be further from the truth! Husbands are not given to us as construction projects. To treat your husband as one is to deny his manhood. If a woman tries to change a man, she will be met with resentment, bitterness and arguments that will never be resolved. The things you would like changed in a man would be better talked out before you marry. Face reality. Talk it out. If your prospective husband does not meet your needs before marriage, he will not after marriage.

Myth #3: I do not need an education, because we will be married forever, and he will provide for me.

About half of today's American school children are raised by single parents, usually by their mothers. Without an education, how can those mothers provide for their children, much less help them with their homework? It takes only a few nights of fourth-grade homework to start unraveling this myth for many a young mother!

Single women usually have the best opportunity of all to get an education and learn a profession. They can be ready to step in if need be and provide an adequate living for their family. This is not a new "pro-woman" attitude. It is as old as history. The Proverbs 31 woman was equal to any task.

Edwin's books for men are read, I believe, by as many women as men. We receive a lot of letters from women as a result. One woman wrote that she was in a dilemma because her husband was unfaithful. She did not know if he loved her, but if they divorced, she could not support herself. Another wrote that her husband abuses her and their children, but she dares not leave because she does not know how to support her family. What a thing to have to consider when your children's welfare is at stake!

These are real situations people like you and me find themselves in every day. Widows, divorcees, senior citizens and even military wives face these struggles. We must act in faith, not fear; however, there is a vast difference between acting in faith and acting on presumption. Presuming you will never need an education is folly.

Myth #4: Men are smarter than women.

This was already disproved sociologically in Chapter 3, but this myth will not hold up biblically, either. Men *and* women have talents and gifts.[8] Do not be intimidated into not using your gifts. Because you marry does not mean God's plan for your life as an individual has ended! Whatever He was leading you into as a single, He may be leading you into as a wife. Keep your eyes and ears open, not just for change but for continuity as well!

When you choose a career, do not let this myth convince you to choose a lesser career than you are capable of doing. Sociologists call women settling for careers below their potential the "Cinderella Syndrome." If you are going to have a career, then choose one that will enable you to be fulfilled and make money. If you need to work, do not live with minimum-wage jobs for the rest of your life if you are capable of more. If your choice is between a low-paying job and an executive salary, choose the executive salary! If your choice is between doing something you enjoy or what is expected of you, do what you enjoy!

Myth #5: My most important goal is falling in love and getting married.

If your "dream" ends at the wedding day, you are forgetting the rest of the marriage with its good and bad times, joys and crises. This myth is exploded by the scripture that says the most important goal of a single woman is to serve the Lord now before she gets busy serving a spouse.[9] If you keep that goal before you at all times, you cannot go wrong. You will truly be seeking first the Kingdom, and everything else will be added to you.[10]

Sarah, Abraham's wife, married a wealthy man with all the prestige that brought, but she lived perhaps the first eighty years of her married life childless, which, in that day, was a disgrace. She was moved from one foreign land to another, and not once—but twice, her husband passed her off as his sister, allowing another man to take her into his harem.[11] Abraham did not seem concerned about her safety but only about his own. God rescued her both times then gave her a son in her old age.

Can you imagine the anguish that must have enveloped Sarah at times? She may have begun her married life thinking, *Now I am going to live happily ever after.* Like each of us, she had to make a lot of adjustments and learn both forgiveness and faith.

If you recognize some of these myths in your life, replace them with this important truth: *If you are not happy single, you will not be happy married.* When you have learned to be happy and victorious, regardless of circumstances, then, in marriage, you will be able to create a happy, victorious, married life for yourself.

Finally, a word to the mothers of this world:

Please do not pressure your daughter into marrying who *you* think is the right one for her. Do pray with her, encourage her to get an education and help prepare her for life. Teach and encourage her to look for a "maximized man." He *is* out there.

Both our daughters married late by most standards. We watched them all through their twenties as one after another of their friends married, had children and some even divorced. Finally, we felt impressed one night to pray for Lois to get married. Edwin, the girls and I agreed in prayer that night. The next morning at law school, a fellow student named Rick Bivins asked Lois to lunch, and they were married just months later.

With Joann, we watched her turn thirty-one with lots of "friends" but still no prospect of marrying. Then one day, she was flying to visit us, and the Lord told her it was time to pray with us about a husband. When she first arrived, she said nothing to us. A few days later, Edwin spontaneously turned to her, and for the first time in her

life, asked if she felt it was time to pray for a husband!
She agreed. They called me into the room, and we prayed
together. Two months later, she became reacquainted with
a college chum, Richard Webster, and they were married
within the year.

Do not get ahead of God!

Remember the story of Isaac and Rebekah, the first
recorded story of "love at first sight"?[12] Abraham sent his
servant to the far home of relatives to find a wife for his
and Sarah's son, Isaac. The servant found a beautiful girl
who agreed to go back with him. It was her choice. When
she saw Isaac as they returned, she jumped off her camel
and went to meet him. Isaac instantly was taken with her,
and they were married.

Isn't that a beautiful love story? The key is that they
were completely in the will of God.

Let God do the choosing.

If you are single, make sure the one you want is the
one God wants you to have as a husband. If you have
Christian parents or family, let them pray with you.
This really is the most important decision you will make
outside of your decision to believe on Jesus Christ and
live for God.

CHAPTER EIGHT

THE "MERGE CRISIS"

EDWIN

Entering and leaving are the basic activities of life.

Entering into marriage, a family, a peer group, corporate life, a sorority or any other assembly, small or large, can be very difficult. Finding acceptance and identity within them can be exhilarating or despairing.

We all have basic social and biological needs, as well as four basic desires we seek to satisfy. The four are: to be, to beget, to belong and to possess. Marriage holds the greatest portent of satisfaction of all our desires and needs. Marriage holds the possibility of becoming the closest thing to a heaven or hell we can experience on earth.

Life is a situation we did not choose; we only choose how to live it. Marriage is one of life's choices. Marriage is choosing to "belong to" and choosing to have the other "belong to" us.

"Belonging" requires a merging of two into one. Scripture reveals that marriage is a covenant relationship. Two people join together as "one flesh,"[1] entering into a union by "belonging" one to another. To retain your own sense of "being" yet give yourself to "belonging" to another creates tension in life—particularly if initial expectations are not met by present realities.

When a woman marries a man, she "merges" herself into him and into an identity with him in marriage. The moment a woman shows her submission in marriage by assuming the man's name, it becomes incumbent on the man to give her a character with which she can be pleased to identify. God's Word says a man is to love his wife as Christ loved the Church and gave Himself for it.[2] Christ provides the Church with identity, security and stability. Husbands are to provide the same for their wives, through love. When those present realities seem to be missing, resentments can unconsciously develop, and a barrier to good relationships can be built as a result of disappointment.

Resolutions depend on revelation. Revelation—in this case, discovering our own attitudes, motives and feelings—always seems more difficult to gain for ourselves than for others. *We have a tendency to judge others by what they do but ourselves by our intentions.* In doing so, we make ourselves to be innocent and others guilty. This is why revelation is necessary or resolutions will be broken.

A woman dreams of a man in terms of the ideal. In courtship, she sees him as the ideal. But on the honeymoon, the clothes come off, underwear is on the floor, hair is left in the sink, the stool lid is up on the toilet, and suddenly, she meets the real as it collides with the ideal. She dreams of him in idealistic terms but marries in reality. The process of adjustment, when reconciling the difference between the two, is critical.

As we said in the first chapter, disappointments in life are not based upon what we find but upon what we expect to find. The gap between the two is the degree of disappointment experienced. Closing that gap is an important issue in merging.

One of the peculiarities of human relationships is that we do not usually discuss the most important things in life, because they are generally the most intimate. To discuss them often requires "dying to self"—killing pride, admitting weaknesses, sharing likes and dislikes, dealing truthfully—and it is painful. Jesus Christ, in Himself, has made it possible for us to have a Mediator,"[3] a "Counselor." He is a "Reconciler"[4] to us and for us. By the very simple expedient of taking a Bible and meditating on the Word with a prayerful heart and open mind, the Lord can minister to us. The answer to every need and problem is to be found in the Word of God.

Merging into "oneness" in marriage, satisfying desires, meeting needs, is lifetime work. *Marriage is an art in which you draw your own portrait.*

Most marriages begin in immaturity. The more immature, the more strain. Inconsistency is a pattern of immaturity, as is the refusal to accept responsibility for our own actions. However, maturity is not absolute but relative and always comparative in life. Chronologically, emotionally, mentally, spiritually, we always are becoming more mature, but we never reach a place of maturity from which we can retire. Maturation is a lifelong process.

Maturity requires commitment; commitments attempted are cause for maturing. Selfishness is a trait of immature childishness. Children can be devastatingly hurtful in their selfishness. So can a woman who refuses to accept responsibility for her own actions and choices, and in her selfishness, refuses to accept the need to "merge."

Crisis is a temporary period of pressurized time which eventually ends. By refusing to accept crisis, one merely prolongs living in the midst of it. "Merging" in marriage is necessary to produce the end result of a new relationship being forged and tempered to last a lifetime. Yet there are women who refuse to merge, and they cause confusion, chaos and crises for everyone around them.

Marriage is only one area where a "merge crisis" can occur. Corporate mergers can be good or bad in the business world, depending on the motives and purposes of those involved in the mergers.

The woman who marries for ulterior or manipulative purposes can be devilish in her motives and actions. Jezebel was one of these. The Bible records that in her marriage to King Ahab, she manipulated him for her own purposes and designs in life.[5] Hers was no crisis in merging but a series of crises created by refusing to merge.

Jezebel was "religious," but she was unrighteous. As the "high priestess" of a pagan cult, her hatred of righteousness was apparent. She desired to annihilate the prophets of God because their prophecies revealed her ungodly and perverse nature. Her neurosis became psychotic when her cult priests were confronted with the marvelous, miraculous and divine intervention by God, on behalf of Elijah, on Mt. Carmel.[6] There was no limit to the evil she intended to do.

The Jezebel spirit is not new to our day. Eve had no such spirit but, nonetheless, was the vehicle Satan used to cause Adam's rejection of God's sovereignty in his life.[7] Women have power with men and, at times, have power over them.

Joseph, as recorded in Old Testament annals, was thrown in jail for making advances to the wife of Potiphar, in whose house he worked. In reality, *he* escaped *her* advances.[8] Potiphar's wife's lust for Joseph tuned to hatred because of his rejection of her. Accustomed to getting her own way and satisfying her lusts in life by manipulating men, she attempted to assassinate Joseph's character by a lie based on circumstantial evidence. Years later, Joseph's vindication was by the truth in which he walked.

Unlike Jezebel, Potiphar's wife was not religious. Hers was a worldly, seductive, manipulative, jealous, haughty and arrogant spirit which desired the man of godly character but only to satisfy her own pleasure. She viewed the relationship with Joseph as a contest, and by his succumbing to her, he was to be a trophy in her showcase of seductiveness. By his sinning, she would be winning. Victoriously she could vaunt her feminine powers with gloating glee before the world. Like Jezebel, she had the spirit of "the spoiler."[9]

Jezebel, however, was religious. She called herself a "prophetess." Centuries later God charged the church at Thyatira with having good works, charity, service and faith but said He had something against them because they allowed "that woman Jezebel, which calleth herself a prophetess, to teach and to seduce my (God's) servants to commit fornication, and to eat things sacrificed unto idols."[10] He gave this "Jezebel" space to repent and she repented not. Because of her refusal to accept His saving grace, God said her children would die so that all would know that He would not suffer the seduction and corruption of His people.[11]

The evil doctrine of "Jezebel" was and is anathema to God and should be to all who know God. Yet, those in the early Church, seeing and hearing what women with the Jezebel spirit did, allowed it to happen with impunity. God deplored the moral cowardice of those who gave tacit approval by ignoring it through the sin of omission.

That same Jezebel spirit is alive and well today. Men, women and churches suffer from it by tolerating it. The tragedy is that governments don't simply condone it but sanction it. Some women today lie unashamedly about men of God and bring false charges that are picked up by others with the same spirit.

There are women who are charming, influential and religious in attitude and aptitude, who curry favor with leaders and, in reality, undermine church leadership by usurping the authority of men in church and at home. They must be dealt with as God deals with them in His Word.

Many a man has been emasculated by a woman whose deception has led him into distraction, which leads to dislocation and eventuates in destruction. These women "merge" in marriage, church membership, jobs and religious organizations for the one purpose of achieving their own agenda. They leave a trail of hurt, woe, division and brokenness behind them as they travel through life.

Theirs is not a crisis in merging but rather crises from refusing to merge.

Like Satan's approach to Eve in the Garden, these women appear to have a desire to help, to show a better way and to make life better, but they appeal to greed while making their actions look divine and helpful. *They offer a messianic promise while performing a satanic service.*

The word for all such women is *repent!*

"A worthy wife is her husband's joy and crown; the other kind corrodes his strength and tears down everything he does."[12]

Marriage is a choice. Merging is a choice.

Your choice for glory or shame.

NANCY

Thank the Lord there are women without the Jezebel spirit! There are those women who are truly attempting to merge with their husbands but find they are having tremendous difficulties. Some women, and men, too, live their lives in marriage as though they were single.

"Help!" a new bride wrote me. "I need your prayers so very much right now. I am having some real problems. I have tried everything, and nothing has helped. One day, everything is great, and my husband tells me how much he loves me. The next day, he is a monster and says he does not love me and does not want to be married after all.

"I get extremely hurt and talk with him then go pray about it. I try not to react, but it has been going on for several months now. Finally, I get upset and leave the house. I come home, expecting to see my bags packed on the doorstep, but instead, there are roses! And he tells me he loves me! I love him with all my heart, but I am having a tough time holding on. Please pray with me. I know God can do miracles."

She did not realize it, but she was in the middle of a "merge crisis," both hers and his. He dealt with the crisis one way, she another.

I knew this couple before they were married and felt pretty sure they were married in the will of God. But regardless of the fact that God puts two people together, the marriage still has to be worked out day by day for a truly successful relationship to grow.

This precious woman did the right thing. She was completely honest before God, taking all the bitter, hurt emotions to Him in private prayer. Toward her husband, she was honest and loving. She confessed her faults as she lovingly confronted her husband with the things he was doing that hurt her. That humility of spirit goes a long way toward keeping a marriage together.

I met this woman some months later, and she was as happy as a new bride is said to be. Instead of allowing resentment to take root, she had discovered how to pray, how to communicate with her husband and how to trust God for the outcome. What had seemed a hopeless situation became the greatest blessing of her life. By submitting herself completely to God, and by persevering, God brought them through the "merge crisis" and into maturity.

Edwin teaches that "crisis is normal to life" and that God takes us through the times of the transient in order to bring us into the permanent. Never is that more true for a woman than in the first months of marriage when she merges with her husband. New husbands, and new fathers, generally react to the merge as well, feeling the full impact of being responsible for another person's life.

I have heard from, and written to, other women who asked for help when they found their husbands were not immediately going to be the leaders in the home or meeters of their needs. These discoveries can lead to deep feelings of hurt, rejection, bitterness and anger toward the husband. If you are one of these women, release those feelings through forgiveness and allow God to intervene in the situation. Even if your merge crisis occurred 25 years ago and you have experienced problems ever since, it is not too late for God to work.

Marriage will not work without effort on your part. Putting all the responsibility on your husband's shoulders, as we have already discussed, is a form of hiding, not submission. You must take the responsibility for your own part in the marriage.

The adjustment to marriage is more difficult when people marry with preconceived notions on how things ought to be—habits formed in other relationships, attitudes, reactions and so forth. No one is completely free from these thoughts. Your husband may be as uncomfortable with what he has found in you as you are with those things you have found in him. So learn to be understanding.

A common complaint today that is far different than brides of fifty years ago is that husbands react negatively to the woman's sexual advances. Brides in days gone by generally felt burdened with their husbands' sexual aggressions. Times change! If you are having trouble in this area, remember that sexual drives are different in each person. Your husband may feel inadequate to fulfill your needs when you act boldly. This may cause him to shy away from you.

Be patient. Cast your burdens on the Lord. Ask His help in the situation. God is a God of specificity. Tell Him your exact problem and believe in faith for the answer. I would encourage you to stay before God until you have the assurance, the "witness" in your spirit, that He has heard you.[13] Then practice patience and understanding with your husband.[14] As you develop a more tolerant and forgiving spirit, your husband may become able to share his own needs, doubts and fears with you.

Stay forgiving and let God use this time to purify and refine you. You can become the wonderful helpmeet God intends for you to be, a wife and mother whose husband and children respect, bless and honor her.

CHAPTER NINE

HELPMEET OR HINDRANCE?

EDWIN

The telephone startled me when it rang. Living on the West Coast near the beach, Nancy and I often get telephone calls in the dark morning hours from people in the East who forget it is three hours earlier for us. This particular morning was cold, foggy and damp.

I was kneeling, my head thrust into the corduroy fabric of the chair in my den, a wool blanket pulled around my shoulders and the sound of my prayers muffled by the thick stuffing. When I answered the phone, a woman's tense, high-pitched voice met my ears. She had called several times before without leaving a telephone number for me to return her call. Now we held an entire conversation without her ever telling me her name or where she was calling from.

Her desperate situation, when all was said and done, was summed up in one statement that expressed her frustration and rage with her husband, her marriage and her life.

She said, "I feel as if I exist just to service him: be his secretary (which she actually was), take his calls, clean his house and give him sex when he desires it. He never wants to talk with me, just plain be with me or show any love. I am an object, not a person."

As she gave me the details of their marriage, I could see the present situation had not always existed, but the marriage had degenerated over the years. What she had failed to see was that much of the condition was due to her own errors in the relationship.

Men feel threatened, women feel guilty. Women tend to give ultimatums, while men make accusations.

She had given him so many ultimatums over the years that he began to avoid any conversation that tended toward confrontation. He was confronted with issues in his business and dealt with them professionally, but he was not able to use the same manner with his wife. Although she desired to deal with issues with her husband as others did, she instead became emotional. Tears in front of others were an embarrassment to him, especially when used as a last resort to get her way with him.

For her, it was her way or no way, but when it became no way, she lost—lost affection, attention and the intimacy that was once hers.

Trying to regain what was lost, she engaged in "nagging" and admitted it. Scripture says it is better to live in the corner of an attic than in a wide house with a nagging wife.[1] She felt like the embodiment of that proverb with a modern appendage, "A man wants a lady in the living room, a secretary in the office, a cook in the kitchen and a whore in the bedroom." Untrue!

The truth is that a man simply wants a woman to be a woman—just as the only thing a woman wants from a man is a man.

I tried to help her as gently but realistically as I could and prayed with her before we hung up. Then I returned to my chair and blanket and thought about the power and energy God has given a woman in relationship to her husband.

One of the hardest things for a man to do is to admit he is wrong.

One of the hardest things for a woman to do is to allow her man to fail.

Men will not always be perfect, nor will they always be successful. Men fail. In their failures, they need neither condemnation nor justification—only acceptance.

Accepting your husband when he is wrong, accepting his weaknesses, accepting his decisions even though you know they will not turn out right, is the measure of your own faith and trust in God.

In most of life, failure precedes success.

The death, burial and resurrection of the vision is a divine principle. Everyone wants the glory of the resurrection, but none want the death that makes it possible. Yet, life is born out of death.

A friend told me in a painfully honest appraisal of herself, that she learned through her husband's mistakes how shaky her faith in God was. She said, "I finally realized I wanted a perfect man so I would not have to trust God anymore."

Men belong to God.

Husbands are stewards of their marriages.

Wives are stewards of their husbands' love.

Love requires trust and acceptance for it to be true love.

The old adage "Behind every successful man is a woman" is often true. However, that does not mean she ran his life to make him successful. More realistically, it implies that she supported him in his failures.

A man from Maine stated in one of our meetings, "I have been afraid of failure and came here today thinking I was a failure. But I believe God has taught me that failing is not the worst thing in the world. Quitting is. And I am not a quitter!" He was on his way to success with that revelation.

Wanting God to change your husband is a valid desire, but a woman must want to change herself to the same extent she wants change in her husband. Women can help change a man's habits. Only God can change a man's nature. When a woman tries to change a man's nature, she takes the place of God. Roadblock and stumbling block: wives are capable of being both.

A young man was told something one day that really shocked him. Mark had just changed churches. It was difficult for him because he loved the pastor and people in his former church, but they were in a spiritually tragic situation. The powerful church board would not allow the pastor to do what God wanted him to do. Therefore, there was no growth and no life in the church. Eventually, Mark decided to go where he could find the life of Christ. What had shocked him was his final conversation with the pastor. Over the years, Mark and his pastor had developed a close relationship, so Mark made an appointment to explain why he was leaving.

When he finished explaining, his pastor leaned toward him with tired eyes and softly said, "I wish I could do the same thing."

Mark was dumbfounded. The pastor explained that leaving would mean moving to a new city, perhaps even changing denominations in order to continue ministering. The move also held the possibility of less income. The pastor was willing, but his wife had made it clear she was not in agreement. She rejected uprooting the children, leaving longtime friends and making a new life at their age. Her final answer to his request to consider it had been "no."

Women whose husbands have to make difficult decisions about their jobs or professions can make it easy or hard, a joy or sorrow, by their attitudes and acceptance— or nonacceptance—of change. I changed areas of ministry three times in six years. Each time was traumatic. What lessened the impact of the change was Nancy's acceptance and attitude.

A wife determines God's will for her family's lives almost secondhand at times. She must believe in her husband's ability to know what is right. She must accept his decision that what he thinks is right for him is also right for her. Sometimes I think it takes more faith for a wife to make changes than it does for a husband. She must trust God in her husband as well as simply trusting God.

A diminutive, energetic woman named Marie testified so graphically to this truth in a conversation with us once. She sat in a restaurant with Nancy and me, eating hors d'oeuvres with her fingers. Her jet-black curls bobbed about her face as she spilled out words in rapid-fire succession. She said her greatest test of faith was not in praying for her own well-being or that of her family or in a time of crisis, but it was when she realized that she had to commit her husband, Jack, to the Lord and trust God to work in his life.

All their married life, Marie had been Jack's support. She had given counsel and advice, whether or not it was requested, and helped him make wise decisions. But she learned she would have to trust God to give Jack wisdom without her help if she wanted him to lead in the home. It was her greatest test, but it became her greatest triumph. When she learned to trust God to work in Jack's life, it liberated her to develop her own character and personality.

With a sigh, Marie paused for a moment and said, "You know, it is great not to have to 'carry him' anymore. I didn't realize how heavy that was. For the first time, I am free!"

It was tough—real tough. But she did it. Jack failed a few times, and they went through some difficult periods, but through them, she learned to trust God in a way she never had before. Trusting Him to work in her husband meant she had to develop her own personal relationship with God. Faith comes by hearing, and hearing by the Word of God.[2]

She said the thing that made it work for her was a daily devotional period. Those times of tears, pouring over the Word and intense prayer meant dying to her own desires and inclinations. From the dying to self came a new life in the Spirit and a new husband. Marie was free to be who she really was, and that allowed Jack to be free, too. Today, he is an international success story.

Are you trusting God to work in your husband? Or are you trying to help God?

God doesn't need your help. He is perfectly capable in Himself of making men.

NANCY

Helpmeet or hindrance—which is it? To me, being a helpmeet implies giving, and being a hindrance implies taking or impeding or being selfish. The Bible tells us to prefer one another in love.[3] This means giving. Well, what are we "giving"?

Let's approach it this way. Sue and Art say their "I do's" at the altar, become husband and wife and go on their honeymoon. Sue suggests they have dinner in their honeymoon suite. Art really does not want to, but he is so much in love that he agrees. The honeymoon is idyllic, then they come home and settle into their new life. Sue comes up with some suggestions, but Art is tired, and he says, "No, I don't want to do that." Then Art wants to do something, but she says, "No way! You don't want to do what I want, so I'm not going to do what you want!"

So begin the struggles of their marriage, one against the other. Sue's attitude is, "If Art won't give in, then I'm not going to either!" This can become an armed-camp situation with each one waiting on the other to capitulate. There is no giving, only taking.

The other question is: To whom are we giving? Some women, when taking on the name "housewife," actually become just that.

Their homes become more important to them than their husbands. As the house takes priority over meeting the needs of the husband, the husband begins to feel he no longer has a wife or a house. So he chooses something else like a garage, garden or boat that can be just the way he wants it.

In a similar situation, many men do not feel like fathers to their own children, because their wives so completely wedge themselves between father and child. These wives may mean well. Perhaps they want to take some pressure off their husbands. But getting between him and the house or the children is bound to become a habit and, later, a chasm.

When the destructiveness of these habit patterns is recognized, there needs to be a release of control and a new, giving attitude, so the husband feels free to come back into the house and family.

Let him make decisions regarding placement of furniture, buying of furnishings and so forth. Perhaps his taste is not as sophisticated as yours or his habits as cultured, but so what! He is your husband and an equal partner in the marriage. He may make mistakes, but so do you. He may not do things exactly as you do them, but he is an *equal partner* in the marriage.

You can give by "giving way" and standing aside for him. This requires godliness within yourself, although a good sense of humor is useful, too! A wife needs to be secure in the fact that God is her Savior, Provider, ultimate "Need-Meeter," that He will look out for her needs and is truly her Source. One of the great traps for any wife is to see her husband, or his job, or her job, as her provider—instead of looking to God to be her ultimate Supplier. When the job or the husband falters, the wife can cripple her husband by her own lack of faith in God.

The ultimate reward of having a Christlike character is peace in the home.[4] You cannot create peace by screaming, *"Will everyone shut up so we can have some peace and quiet around here?"* You can have quiet that way for a while, but it will not be a peaceful hush. It will be a tense quiet, just waiting for another eruption. Peace is what you bring to your home through righteousness, because righteous living brings peace. Do not lose your peace over your husband! Keep your peace, regardless of what happens, and be a true help to him, not a hindrance.

I asked Edwin what I meant to him as a "helpmeet." He replied that what stands out in his mind was arriving home from a long, hard day at the office, or from visiting among the congregation, to find a tidy, clean home with dinner nearly always on the table. Also, I did not run to meet him at the door with all the calamities of the day, ready to unsettle him for the evening.

Now, I have never considered myself a perfect house-keeper. I have always been comfortable with a little dust on the furniture and a few dishes in the sink. But the overall picture to Edwin was that I had things under control and was providing for him and the children. I enjoyed having a family to care for, and I was always concerned about nutrition and providing balanced meals. So whether or not I was working outside the home at the time, I personally saw to it that my children were well fed.

On the other hand, Edwin did not come home to be "lord of the manor"! I tried to give him at least 20 minutes to start unwinding. Then, often he helped with anything I needed from vacuuming to doing the dishes—and he still does.

He was and is willing to help me (and I am the same with him). Because of that, the esteem he held me in was reciprocated. He did not demand respect, but because he treated me with care and consideration, it was easy to see his likes and dislikes and see that they were taken care of.

You may say, "I wish I had a husband like that, but my husband is a regular terror. He insists on certain things which I am just not going to provide!"

Let me ask you something: Is he asking something that would compromise your faith? If he is, do not do it. But if he is asking for something you could do, but you are holding back, then by all means—do it![5] As we *give* of ourselves in a relationship, we teach our husbands how to give. Your husband may never have had a living example of giving. But if you show him what true love and giving are, tremendous harmony can be produced.

I thought the self-centeredness of the "Me-Generation" was gone, but it still seems to crop up almost everywhere. Recently, a woman wrote who had married and had three children within six years. During that time, she discovered her husband could not, or would not, do the household accounts, so she had to do them. He did not help with the children, which she resented. Now he had asked her to help in his business. She was incensed at this and was ready for divorce, feeling it was the last straw.

I answered her letter as gently as I could, trying not to demean her. A vivid picture of our forebears came to my mind. The women then had no labor-saving devices. They made their own soaps and candles, toted buckets of water from the well, washed clothes on a scrub board and ground their own wheat. Many helped their husbands with the livestock and in the fields as well. In addition, they bore and raised eight to ten children.

I would never want to go backwards to that time, and I am not belittling housework today, but if I had lived in those days, I would have expected those discomforts. Edwin says disappointments come because we expect something different from what we get. The point is, it is not the amount of work—but your attitude—that determines whether or not you help your husband.

A wise preacher once said, "We have only as much religion as we have in times of emergencies." When all is going according to our expectations, we can pray in victory and believe we have a calm and peaceful spirit. But when things do not fit our plans, we either have to make adjustments, fall apart or go to our knees. Sometimes, God has other plans! He may want to use our husbands, or even our children, in a way we were not prepared for. Yielding to His will makes life so much more peaceful.

The woman who wrote me needs to understand that if she will willingly give her husband the help he needs now, then someplace down the road, he will be singing her praises to all who will listen. He will be telling them what a wonderful wife he has and admitting what he may have done wrong.

Helpmeet or hindrance—which will it be for you? A woman can hinder a man in many ways, throwing cold water on his new business idea or not wanting to move when there is a chance of advancement.

About fifteen years ago, we met a couple who had just moved to our community. The first time I met Janet, I was impressed with her grace, social skills and lightness of spirit. Since then, they have made four major moves, moving hundreds of miles in each direction.

Yet I have never heard Janet complain about moving, about going from a warm climate to a cold one, or even moving overseas. I have never seen her hesitate about leaving behind friends or beautiful homes, although certainly it must not have been easy. Instead, she finds beauty in every situation. I have visited her in almost every locale where they have resided, and I know from firsthand experience that this is true.

Whenever they move, Janet immediately becomes involved in a local church which usually provides her with instant friendships. Today, in a new home with yet another circle of friends, Janet is optimistic. Even though the tragic death of a grandson has occurred, Janet looks to the future with hope because God is her Source, her Hope and her Future.

Helpmeet or hindrance?

A woman wrote, wanting to know what Edwin and I thought about her asking her husband to quit his job which often took him away from home. Even when he was home, he went hunting with his father. Also, he worked with non-Christians, and she was afraid they would be a bad influence. My reply to her, in part, was like this:

"Be very careful about asking your husband to change jobs. Pray extensively about it first. Is it the Lord's will? Or is it yours because of lack of faith? You have no assurance his next job would keep him home more or offer a better atmosphere. You could send him into an even worse situation. Really, it does not matter where he works, because there are temptations everywhere—even in a Christian environment.

"You need to start working on you. Spend more time in the Word and prayer. Do not expect instant miracles. (But don't turn them down if they come!) Repent of any animosity or resentment you have.[6] Release him through forgiveness. Might I also suggest spiritual warfare? The devil really does go around seeking whom he may devour.[7] But we have an Advocate with the Father—Jesus Christ.[8]

"The devil would like to devour you with fear and devour your marriage. But what has Jesus done? He has overcome the world, the flesh and the devil! Hurt grows when you nurture it. It can get to be a big, ugly thing. That is the reason couples divorce after fifteen, twenty or even twenty-five years of marriage. The problems festered there for a long time until they became unbearable and caused the split.

"You need to daily invoke the Name of Jesus in prayer to guard and protect your husband and your family. God answers the effectual fervent prayer of the righteous, and He is the Rewarder of those who diligently seek Him.[9] I hope this helps you. We will be praying for you."

With that, I concluded the letter. And with that, I conclude this chapter. I hope this helps you, too!

CHAPTER TEN

WISE WIVES AND HARDENED HUSBANDS

EDWIN

Modern society sees "self as God." That philosophy is the core of humanism and began in the Garden of Eden when Eve saw that the fruit of the tree was "good."[1] She did not realize that her desire to eat of it was "evil." By transgressing the commandment, both she and Adam denied God's right of sovereignty in their lives.

God has a sovereign right to say what is good and evil, to command to partake or abstain. God has a twofold right to man, both by creation naturally and re-creation spiritually in Christ. Sin basically is a denial of God's right of possession.

The devil's strategy is to divide. God's strategy is to unite. Satan separated man from God by tempting him to sin. God united man with Himself by redeeming him from sin.

Today the devil's strategy still is to separate men from God, husbands from wives, parents from children, and to destroy relationships and lives.[2] Thank God, the purpose of Christ's coming was and is to destroy the works of the devil.[3] God's purpose and desire are to bring dignity and unity to marriage. To accomplish that, Christ had to pay the penalty for sin by death on Calvary, and then be raised from the dead to make possible our right standing with God and oneness with Him. That is the wisdom of God.

There are two classes of men—saved and unsaved. They live in two different kingdoms. The unsaved live in the kingdom of Satan and the saved in the Kingdom of God. Conversion is God's process of bringing us from the kingdom of darkness into the Kingdom of Light through the New Birth.

Walking in two different kingdoms when united in marriage is difficult at best. Satan is the "father of lies," Christ is "Truth."[4] The spirit of each is diametrically opposed to the other. The Bible calls it being "unequally yoked."[5]

Where "self is Lord," selfishness is the rule.

Where "God is Lord," selflessness is the rule.

Married couples who live in different kingdoms and later are united in Christ are blessed beyond measure, but such marriages are more the exception than the rule. Nancy and I are one of those exceptions. When I met her, I was a rabid worldling. One look at her, and I loved her, *really* loved her. But that did not stop my worldly ways. She was a religiously devout, morally correct, culturally couth and naturally gracious young woman. Why she ever married me, I will never know, but she did, thank God! Two years later, I experienced a glorious conversion. Boy, was I saved! My whole life changed instantly, then was being changed constantly. My transition from a confirmed worldling to a conformed Christian was dramatic and traumatic.

Nancy was "religious" and deeply committed to her church, but she was not converted to Christ because she had never accepted Christ as her Lord. Suddenly, we lived in two different kingdoms and were miles apart in our approach to life. The chasm deepened as I left her at home while I pursued faithful attendance at church. I loved her more than ever, but neither of us knew what to do about the growing distance.

Concerned with the widening rift, I sought counsel. Good and well-meaning people recommended to tell her nothing, make her curious and then, when she asked questions, I could tell her about my newfound relationship with the Lord. Wrong! She did not ask, and I did not share, waiting for her to ask.

Those people gave me "advice" but not godly counsel. The difference can mean Heaven or Hell, marriage or divorce. The advice actually drove us further from each other.

More deeply concerned than ever, I did what I should have done from the beginning: I sought God during a time of fasting and prayer.

One day while on the job, I asked Him again what to do. This time His counsel to me was almost audible: "Tell her everything!" With it came the assurance that she would come to know Him as I did. That night I rushed home, dirty work clothes and all, with the exciting news of the day. In my human zeal, I almost killed a spiritual birthing.

When I said, "Nancy, God has promised to save you, and I am to tell you everything," it went over like a lead balloon. However, I did tell her.

Weeks later, we knelt across from each other beside our bed and prayed that God would make us one before the birth of our first child. We agreed in prayer, she believing I would become a member of her faith, and me knowing what God had told me. She began to attend meetings with me and even studied her Bible.

Finally, just a month before Paul was born, Nancy was standing at her ironing board when, in her words, "the presence of the Holy Spirit entered the room." She set the iron down, lifted her eyes and said, "Lord, I believe." That glorious day, she passed from death unto life.

Now living in the same Kingdom, we had the same mind, the same Spirit and the same Counselor. Were it not for Him, I doubt we would be married today. If nothing else, my worldly, selfish, pleasure-seeking ways would have destroyed the marriage.

The advice I received from well-meaning friends was wrong, and it almost cost me my wife and marriage. Godly counsel consists of divine truth with practical applications. I needed the wisdom of God to give me a strategy to obtain a victory in our marriage for the glory of God.

"Wisdom is the principal thing; therefore get wisdom: and with all thy getting get understanding."[6] Wisdom is the greatest need you have in your life. Wisdom gives a long, good life; riches; honor; pleasure; peace.[7]

Knowledge is the acquiring of facts, understanding is the interpreting of facts, but wisdom is the application of facts.

Knowledge is not enough—you need wisdom.

There are two kinds of wisdom. The wisdom of this world is "earthly, sensual, devilish"[8] and is the reason there is such confusion, misunderstanding and war in the world. The wisdom of God has the characteristics of the nature of God and makes for peace. You cannot resolve conflicts between light and darkness with worldly wisdom. Psychology may be relevant to the day in which we live, but if it is not applied according to the Word of God, it will result only in confusion and chaos. You need godly wisdom which comes only from the Word of God by the Spirit of God.

The fear of the Lord is the restraint from doing evil.[9] Where there is no fear of the Lord, there is no restraint. The fear of the Lord is the beginning of wisdom, because the beginning of wisdom is to depart from evil.[10] Satan has knowledge but not wisdom, because he has no fear of the Lord.

He who has the fear of the Lord and the wisdom of God has dominion over the devil. Jesus was manifested that He might destroy the works of the devil.[11] He is made unto us wisdom, righteousness, sanctification and redemption.[12] His wisdom destroys the devil's works which is why we need wisdom.

If we lack wisdom, we are to ask of God, Who promises to give it without measure.[13] God has all knowledge. He is not partial, either in favoritism or in completeness. We are partial. We cannot see everything completely. We are blighted and cannot see or understand perfectly; however, we are wise when we trust in a living God Who is perfect, complete, and has all knowledge and wisdom. When we trust God, we are wise. Refusing to trust is to lack faith and be without wisdom. Not to trust God is dumb!

Evidence of our lack of wisdom is found in the use of substances that can kill us. When God created man and woman and placed them in the Garden, He gave them dominion over the earth, including all plant life. Today, in our perverted world, plant life is taking dominion over mankind. Beer, alcohol, marijuana and cocaine are derived from plants which are making "users" of men instead of men using plants.

Satan is called the "father of lies" by the Lord Jesus Christ,[14] which is why the assessment is true that all adulterers, alcoholics, abusers and addicts are liars. You must realize this axiomatic principle and accept it as fact to be able to deal with such men (or women). To deny it, hide from the truth of it or attempt to avoid it is to run away from any solution to the problem.

Women who marry men with obvious problems, thinking they can change them after marriage, are deceiving their own hearts. "All he needs is the love of a good woman" is the classic statement of women who marry alcoholics and then live to regret it. All a man really needs is God. A good woman can help—but a man needs God!

The one overriding need of a woman married to an abuser or user is the wisdom of God to know how to deal with the man and the situation in which she finds herself. Someone once told me this kind of marriage is similar to being a Daniel in a lion's den. A lion is an irrational creature. The lion's roar is so frightening, it literally paralyzes its victim with fear, which makes it easy prey for the lion. The Bible says Satan goes about "as a roaring lion...seeking whom he may devour."[15] The simile is to teach us we are not to fear and become prey to the devil, but take dominion over him.

Our "lions' dens" are irrational thoughts, emotions and motives. The "lions" that would destroy us are jealousy, envy, anger, hate, malice, vengeance, greed, strife, spite, criticism and such things. However, God shut the lions' mouths for Daniel,[16] and He can do the same for us.

I met a woman named Julie in Tampa who told me about finding out her husband was having an affair. It almost crushed her. The lions were roaring. But while seeking God, she was impressed to go to her husband, look him in the eye and tell him, "You are God's gift to me. I love you." That closed the mouths of the "lions" of murder, anger, hate, despair and divorce. The Word of God produced the spirit of a Daniel. God saw Julie through her night in the lions' den. Her husband became convicted of his sin and eventually repented.

On the other hand, when Abigail's husband, Nabal, whom the Bible calls a "fool," arrogantly denied King David's request, Abigail knew he was wrong. Having lived with him, she knew upbraiding him would have no effect. Instead, she took the offering to David. Her faith, which was her belief in action, stopped David from destroying Nabal's household. Nabal died a "fool's" death, but Abigail became the wife of a king.

Married to a "fool," a woman may not always see her husband saved, but she can save herself and her family by her right relationship with God.

My counsel to women married to men not serving God is to avoid the mistake of trying to compete with the "sex symbols" of the world. *Exterior beauty cannot compare with internal loveliness.* God's admonition is to adorn your spirit with attitudes of reverence, meekness, quietness and peace.[17]

Also, do not insist on "your way" or "no way" at all. Given the ultimatum, a man usually will choose "no way" at all. Rejection is the result. Take what you can get and use it to personal advantage. Be creative in ways to show love. Ask God for a strategy.

Do not force your husband to talk your kind of talk—especially "Jesus talk"—if he is not interested. A common complaint of wives is a husband's lack of communication. How can she know what to do, or how to do it, if he won't talk? With demands, you raise barriers, instead of tearing them down. The barriers that need breaking are predisposition, preconception and predetermination. They cannot be overcome by force. You cannot talk to a man about the Lord if he will not communicate. So, prime the pump. Be willing to give, even in communication. Become interested in what interests him. When listening to him, do not interrupt, correct or challenge him. If you know he is wrong, let him be wrong. It will not hurt you.

Do not tell your husband things about yourself by way of accusation, saying he should have known them already. Instead, let it be a discovery to him. Accusations will silence him quicker than anything.

God's wisdom can give you a strategy for victory in your marriage. God's strategy is far different than manipulation.

It is the wisdom of God that if a man has war in his heart, stay away; if battered by him, leave; if betrayed, love; if persecuted, pray. The highest good for any man is unity in Christ. To obtain either, the wisdom of God is needed. When you pray for wisdom, God will give you a strategy whereby you obtain the victory in the warfare, and the glory of God is the result.

Begin now—ask God for wisdom.

Wisdom is the principal thing.

NANCY

A woman who read one of Edwin's books was stricken by what he said to men. The elements of courage, acceptance of responsibility, sensitivity to a wife's needs—these all seemed beyond the scope of her life and her husband's.

She wrote to ask, "Can *my* husband really acquire these attributes?"

The answer is YES! No one is beyond the reach of our powerful God and the precious Holy Spirit. But what are you looking forward to in your life? Do you want a handsome movie idol to sweep you off your feet and carry you off to a fantasyland where you will live happily ever after, with no problems, no struggles and no worries? If so, I need to tell you—life is not like that!

God will transform a man from "glory to glory"[18]—in other words, cause him to be conformed to the image of Christ, but you need to accept him as he is, as he grows. Just as you have strengths and weaknesses, so does your husband or future husband.

Starting with simpler problems, cultural differences alone are enough to put strain on a marriage. One of the adjustments Edwin and I had to make was concerning food. Although he was raised in California, his mother was from Texas, and she brought up her family on that wonderful Southern cooking—black-eyed peas, cornbread, biscuits and gravy, turnip greens, buttermilk and chicken-fried steak.

I grew up in New England on johnnycake, baked beans and brown bread, steamed clams, oyster stew and all the wonderful foods of that region. Much of what was "normal" to me was not to Edwin and vice versa. To make matters worse, neither of us had cooked much before we got married. To his credit, he never criticized my cooking. Gradually, I developed a healthy appreciation for the food of the South and Southwest, and he grew to like New England cuisine as well.

Another cultural difference was in the habit of expressing affection. My family never touched, hugged or kissed anyone while Edwin's family was the touching, kissing, hugging kind. This, at first, produced problems much bigger than food differences.

So it will be in your home until you are able to understand and accept your husband as he is and work patiently and tolerantly toward a perfect union. This will become easier as you pray that God would make of your mate exactly what He wants. If you pray for your husband to change simply to make your life easier, there is an element of selfishness involved; but if you are praying for his highest good with pure motives, God can answer in ways you have not dreamed of.

Another difference you may run into is in the expression of anger. If you were brought up in a gentle, loving home where you were never yelled at and rarely spanked, and your mate has known harsh, perhaps violent, correction, you can be in for some traumatic times. There are other homes where resentments are fostered but hidden. Instead, they come out in hateful attitudes and dislikes, even against close relatives. Surmounting these difficulties in marriage and child rearing is a task we must give daily to the Lord in prayer, asking His wisdom in every difficulty. Your attitude will stem from either a soft heart or a hard heart. A soft heart attuned to God through prayer and study of the Word will be able to give "a soft answer" that "turneth away wrath."[19]

Many times we can turn a crisis around by using the wisdom God so willingly wants to give us. I remember when the words about wisdom that are found in the eighth chapter of Proverbs made their first impact on me. "Doth not wisdom cry? and understanding put forth her voice?"[20] Was God saying that "wisdom" was crying out to *me*, Nancy? I thought I was the one who had to do all the work! But God is calling to us,[21] desiring to give us wisdom and to keep us from falling on the hard places of life, that we might live in the "fullness of joy" He has promised.[22] A good reading assignment would be the first nine chapters of Proverbs which all concern wisdom.

A troubled wife wrote to us concerning her husband who had told her he was having an affair. He was "praying" about whether to stay married to her. Apparently, he did not realize that marriage is a sacred covenant, established by God, whereby two people become one. The Bible says to let no man put asunder what God has joined together.[23]

This husband had broken his covenant by infidelity; therefore, his prayers were going to have little effect on God until he repented of his adultery.[24] I wrote to this woman to go before the Lord in repentance and humility of heart and ask Him to give her wisdom to sustain her, comfort her and guide her in the days ahead. Forgiving her husband was the next most important thing to do.[25] Seeking wise counsel from a pastor or others should come after that.

Another woman wrote, "We have been married seventeen years. My husband physically abused me and the children for ten years, even threatening us with guns. This situation created rebellion, anger, disobedience and low self-esteem in us all. I left him after I accepted Christ, but a pastor's wife persuaded me to go back to him. A year later, he also accepted Christ, and we did great for awhile, even attending church. But the children were much older, and problems began to surface. Since he had never learned to deal with the children in love, or to deal with his own feelings, once again, he began to threaten us. All the old reactions surfaced, and soon, the family just exploded. The kids resorted to alcohol and drugs, and one became very violent. That is where we are now. You are the first person I have heard talk about things like this. What should I do?"

I realize this is not an unusual occurrence, unfortunately. What goes on in some Christian homes would shock many people—unless they have seen it behind their own doors. If you are being physically abused, you prayerfully need to leave that home. Many women get to the point where they are convinced they deserve the abuse—but that is never true. No one does! Living in a state of abuse is a violent, abnormal way to live, not only outside the norms of society, but definitely outside the norms of Christian living. Remember, your body is the temple of the Holy Spirit[26] and should not be abused by anyone in any way. If there are children involved, it is all the more reason to get them out of that desperately unhappy and dangerous situation. You may still love the man and want to see him change, but you cannot expose yourself and your children to those circumstances.

Your husband may not be abusive, but there may be other things in his life that grieve you. God is the "God of the impossible." You do not know what He wants you to do until you ask Him! Even when the situation seems impossible, perhaps from marrying in haste, take it all to the Lord in prayer!

Bitterness or resentment toward your predicament will have to be dealt with first. Before you can deal with your husband's defects, you have to deal with your own.[27] Forgive and release the other's sins out of your own life. Without that release, you carry a heavy burden. But Jesus said His yoke is easy and His burden is light.[28]

Go to work on yourself! Change can come in an instant, but usually, we have to work on things day by day. So, give yourself a spiritual briefing:

Are you working out your own salvation in fear and trembling?[29]

Is your attitude forgiving?

Is your spirit bringing a peaceful, godly atmosphere into your home?

Are you holding grudges against family members?

Seek the Lord. Join a Bible study group. Share one another's burdens (without resorting to gossip). Somehow, praying for someone else's misfortune seems either to change our perspective of our own or to give us the strength to go on.

Work on that peaceful spirit! Read Proverbs 31, Isaiah 30:15 and Psalm 23 daily. Make a list of verses on quietness, rest and peace, and read them aloud daily.

When children are involved, find *godly* counsel for them. There is a great deal of human wisdom available that does not hold a candle to a *godly* counselor who approaches the task with wisdom that comes from God.

Bury yourself in the Word. It is a mirror that enables us to see ourselves as we are and to gain insight into the issues at hand. The Bible really is an eternally current and "modern" book. It answers every question that can be raised with the wisdom of the ages.

Here is a letter we received after a woman saw tremendous changes in her marriage:

"A few weeks ago, I saw you (Edwin) on television and wept as you spoke on the truth about forgiveness. I can't tell you the balm that ministered to my wounded soul. My husband was hurt when helping to found a church. In anger, he turned against it, although we have never left.

"His bitterness has caused untold suffering to me and my children. He got worse and worse, and after forty years of marriage, I was ready to throw in the towel. But he went to one of your meetings—which he did *not* like—and I read your book. Then I got your tapes and began to listen to them with earphones every night, praying for God to put those qualities you ministered into my husband's life.

"Things actually have begun to change for the better! He has a way to go, but now he cannot tell me enough how much he loves me! This seemed impossible before. Although he did not like your meeting, I believe God used it to begin to break through his hard heart. When you prayed for those women on television, I wept for so many women across this land who were watching. What healing! Young and old alike need to hear it."

This gracious woman is a model to every woman who is facing the difficulties of marriage to a hardened husband. From her perspective of forty-plus years of marriage, please receive this teaching to forgive and pray for your husband and seek wisdom from God for your marriage.

CHAPTER ELEVEN

DON'T DIE
AT HOME

EDWIN

What is wrong with being a mother?

What is wrong with taking pleasure in the raising of a family?

Why should a woman feel guilty because she takes pleasure in providing a peaceful, serene, orderly home, raising her children in the fear of the Lord and being devoted to God and family?

Today's secular Pharisees who justify their every inconsistency have stigmatized the devoted mother. "Housewife" has become a hissing byword to the arrogant socio-engineers of our day. Motherhood is acceptable to them only in the context of a "broader, fulfilled life," where the woman balances it with lovers, career and success.

God says He hates "those who say that bad is good, and good is bad."[1] He probably hates none more than those who pervert the true meaning of life in order to justify their own failures, satisfy their own angers or take vengeance for their hurts.

Today's family is the womb of tomorrow's society, and today's parents are those who impregnate it with the seeds of the future.

Today's parents face a different societal flux, suffer unique stress, contend with moral change and fight cultural patterns that were not even considered a few years ago.

Economic conditions are making "working parents" the norm for our day which is forcing a readjustment of concepts held dear a generation ago. Men, as well as women, are having to learn to balance working and caring under powerful new pressures. A piano string needs tension for fine-tuning, but when the pressure is too great, it snaps. That "snap" in people is a breakdown emotionally, morally, familially, economically and spiritually, resulting in divorce, drugs and disease.

Sitting on the breakfast table in most American homes have been milk cartons with the pictures of children lost, stolen or kidnapped. Not a pleasant way to start the day. American parents now fingerprint their children, videotape them, implant radio sensors in their teeth or send them to classes where they are taught how to beware of and deal with strangers. Horror stories of child care centers abound, making parents susceptible to more fear and paranoia concerning their children. Children are raised with fear, suspicion and distrust.

Sports, at one time, were just that—sports. Today, they are "competitions." The pressure on boys and girls to perform, excel and exceed is new to our day. Yesterday, it was enough just to participate, but today you have to win. Everything for the winner, nothing for the loser. Losing is not acceptable, much less respectable. The days of teaching "fair play" are gone. Teaching your child to respect the rights of others is out of fashion. Temper tirades by champion athletes on television have set examples for young boys and girls learning how to play.

Lying, cheating, stealing, because they are not punished, have become acceptable traits.

Children who are given to babysitters during the day and have to adjust to parents in the evening and on the weekend can become confused by the conflicting value systems confronting them from the "authority figures" in their lives.

Drugs are like candy today: available, enjoyable and tempting to surfeiting. The medical profession may decry the "drug culture," yet doctors have helped create it with prolific prescriptions and the use of drugs. Parents dealing with drug abuse in their children are not warring against flesh and blood but against diabolical demonic forces.[2] As unclean spirits are the progenitors of pornography, so drugs and terrorism derive from demonic activity.

Parents must learn to deal with it all. Parenting is a learned ability, and learning will involve mistakes.

The good news is, there is wisdom from a loving Heavenly Father for dealing with your children. And there is a grace and faithfulness from God that is more than able to compensate for your mistakes.[3] It did for mine.

Nancy and I have three children. We are grateful to God for them and their achievements, but our gratitude knows no bounds for their personal salvation and love for the Lord Jesus Christ. Their salvation is our greatest source of satisfaction regarding them. The Apostle John wrote, "I have no greater joy than to hear that my children walk in truth."[4]

However, I must admit, as much of an influence I may have been or tried to be, Nancy's influence upon our children has had a powerful effect. The ultimate accolade of her life is to hear the Lord say, "Well done." But approximating that accolade on earth is to hear the children rise up and call her "blessed."[5] And they have.

We look back over our lives and realize with such fervent appreciation the grace of God that compensated for our errors with our children. None of us will ever be without the mistakes, but oh!—the joy of the retrospective look to see where the grace of God made the difference.

An absolutely vital element in parenting, which we learned over the years, is the unity and agreement between the parents. It is not uncommon in men's meetings for me to look at the men, eyeball to eyeball, and tell them pointedly, "Never, never, never disagree with your wife in front of the children, for when you do, you lose authority over them." Likewise, when the mother disagrees with the father, neither wins; both lose.

We have evidence of this principle with the people building the "tower of Babel." *The place of agreement is the place of power.* Disagreement always results in powerlessness. Children are master psychologists and are the number one cause of arguments in the home. They know instinctively that if they can get Mom and Dad into disagreement, they can take over the authority of the home.

Agreement between the parents as to what values are to be instilled is vital. Teaching children to discern between good and evil takes more effort in a society where the moral level is constantly degenerating. Take the case of a marriage marred by the inability to develop good interpersonal relationships because of an addiction to television. Communication skills are impaired, and unity and singleness of purpose never develop properly. This causes the weakness that leads to the fracture of the marriage and the home. Children become the issue in the struggle and are more susceptible to immoral influences than moral.

Three things are vital to normalcy of home life: intimacy, discipline and love. Love is necessary, but discipline is absolutely vital. Discipline is based on correction, not punishment. Where there is no love, there is merely legalism. Punishing sons and daughters for doing something wrong, when the parent has not first taught them how to do it right is, in itself, wrong.[6] Mediocre men want authority, not accountability. They abandon discipline and decisions in the home, so if they are wrong, they can blame someone else. They do not realize the sin of omission is the basic sin of humanity.

Moms—working moms, single moms, stepmoms, tired moms—are trying to handle it all. One lady wrote me:

"The women in our family have always done 99.9 percent of the child rearing, household management, chores and work in their marriages. 'Supermom' has been in existence for years. Of my thirty-five cousins, the girls were given more responsibilities than the boys who generally just took out the trash. As a watcher of Christian television, I have noticed that when child rearing is brought up, generally the problems are blamed on a permissive society and Women's Lib, and the solution given is for mothers to stay at home.

"Mr. Joe Smith never gets addressed! However, Mrs. Joe Smith is admonished to raise the children, stay at home and be submissive to her husband as head of the house. Thus, Christian television perpetuates the matriarchal society and family."

She has a point. Not just some on Christian television, but many in the Church, give the mother the bulk of the responsibility for the child. The same perversion that erroneously says marriage is a fifty-fifty proposition is also wrong concerning the children. Marriage is a hundred-hundred proposition. There is no holding out for self in a marriage. Neither is there room for men to refrain from responsibility toward the children, thinking it is women's work. The more you do what your husband does not do, the more he will let you, and the more stress you will suffer. Do not assume his mantle. Agree on your responsibilities.

There is no reason for ignorance in today's society. There is too much information available. The problem is not lack of information. The problem is that too few read, and too many want only entertainment. Entertainment can be as much a drug as anything else. It, too, is a way of escape.

At times, I have read through women's magazines on airplanes as I travel. They give me an understanding of what women in the world are thinking which helps me realize what the Gospel and committed Christians are facing today. I have found, however, that most women's magazines deal with relationships and self-help, while most men's magazines deal with business and recreation. Very little in men's magazines is written to help them, guide them and educate them in their relationships. Most of that education is in books, not magazines, so the man who habitually reads magazines instead of books misses basic information he desperately needs.

Men think they know about relationships intuitively— and generally don't.

Sons generally learn from fathers and daughters from mothers. It is a wise mother who compensates for what the father omits, but chances are, you married a man whose mother did not. As a result, so often it falls to the woman to try to teach the man what he needs to know. That is a hard task, requiring the utmost wisdom and proficiency.

Nancy helped teach me.

"Paul's upset because he didn't make the team; could you talk to him?" she would inform me.

"Lois isn't doing well in History; I think she could use your help."

"Joann's friend was mean to her today; can you encourage her?"

These were neither naggings nor corrections. They were simply showing me how to pick up on cues that Nancy had already learned to discern.

I learned the "principles of intercession" from an internationally-known teacher, Joy Dawson. She taught me things about prayer I had never known, and she challenged me to practice them. The deep intimacy Nancy and I now have came from applying those principles. They changed my life and my marriage. When we practiced them together, it brought us an intimacy and unity that I never dreamed possible.

Prayer produces intimacy.

Those principles enabled Nancy and me to pray earnestly and in agreement for our children in their hours of crisis. To this day, I believe it was intercessory praying that protected our son and daughters and kept them during the difficult times of their lives.

Intercession is a form of dying to self, which is why so few seem to practice it. Prayer is ministry.

Ministry is not simply standing up speaking to people. Ministry is serving. Preparing meals, making beds and cleaning house are all acts of ministry. Recognizing them as ministry, rather than chafing about "the chores," makes life easier. Women who regard mothering as ministry take joy and delight in what they do.

The dinner hour is a time when there should be minimal stress. It is a ministry hour for every member of the family, single mothers included. However, in many homes, meals occur in shifts, are gulped while watching television or are created with a quick trip to a fast food dispenser (I do not call them restaurants). Sterile relationships from noncommunication develop as a result, and an opportunity for ministry is missed.

The dinner table is generally the one place a mother is in complete control. Making the dinner hour a time of ministry, fixing a good meal and setting a pleasant table is an art. Teaching correct table manners and establishing standards of behavior are a vital part of "limit-setting" in children's lives.

Failure to set limits is fatal to good behavior. The dinner hour is a vital time to guide family lives. "Redeeming the time" is an exhortation of Scripture, and it applies to the totality of life.[7] Do not squander a valuable resource for training.

Ministering to your husband also takes on more than one dimension. Creating an image during courtship was part of your ministry. Destroying it after marriage by failing to maintain it is the height of folly. Scripture says we can ruin our chances by our own foolishness and then blame it on God.[8] Taking a wife for granted is the man's failure in ministry. Letting him do it is hers.

How do you look in the morning and when going to bed at night? How do you act when separating in the morning and reuniting in the evening?

If he travels, do you have a warm welcome and warm bed to meet him with, or do you meet him with preoccupied attitudes and complaints? Lonely men on lonely nights in lonely hotel rooms anticipate and meditate on what they are coming home to. It needs to be both pleasurable and desirable.

Ralph and Esther were like a second set of parents to me. I worked for Ralph and even stayed at his house occasionally. Once while there, I returned home before Ralph and went to my room. Later, when he came home and Esther served dinner, I noticed she had changed clothes, was well made up and perfumed.

When I inquired, she laughed and said that was the secret of their marital longevity. Whether or not she worked, she always prepared herself for the evening with her husband. By doing so, she kept the friendship and romance alive for their four decades of marriage.

Billie Burke, who was married to the famed Flo Ziegfeld, was asked by a newspaper reporter how she had managed to stay married to him when he was surrounded by so many gorgeous women. She said she always rose before he did and made herself ready for the day before he came to breakfast. In the evening, she was at her finest and never took off her makeup until he was asleep. Extreme measures but it was an extreme situation.

Is it hard work? Yes!

Is it ministry? Yes!

Is it worth it? Yes!

By maintaining their image of femininity and loveliness, these women maintained their relationships.

Not only your husband, but your children take great pride in their mother and the way she looks. Establish the image, then maintain it. You will know the value of your efforts when you hear them say, "That's my wife" or "That's my mom" with appreciation in their voices.

Proper planning is also ministry.

Women who do not manage their time well will always produce stress in family life. Time is the only commodity in life that, when expended, can never be recaptured. You can gain back health and wealth but not time. Once gone, it is gone forever. The successful wife and mother is an expert in time management. She plans her days both present and future.

Nancy carries a "Filofax" with everything necessary written in it. She knows what, when, where and how. We meet together regularly to go over our calendar, to keep current with both our activities and needs. The principle is: *What people do not understand they are against.* Keeping others informed and scheduled reduces stress and tension.

When the children were young, we held what we called "family council." This was not devotional time but a time where we set our agendas, revised responsibilities, updated our activities and even voted on what we would do or where we would go. The children's votes counted as much as mine or Nancy's. Of course, we let them vote only on things which were of interest to us all, but we did abide by the vote once it was taken. My veto power was used very, very sparingly.

Set your calendar months in advance. Plan your vacations and trips years in advance. They become goals to work toward. Meet with your husband regularly to update yourselves on time, finances, goals and desires. If he can do it with his secretary, boss or foreman at work, he can do it with you.

Organize your home. Run it efficiently. Inefficiency creates tension and waste. Give family members responsibilities and see that they do them. Your success depends on how you do it. A gentle reminder beforehand is better than creating guilt afterwards. You may have to remind everyone when birthdays, anniversaries and family occasions are coming up, but better to swallow your pride and remind them than become a martyr when dates are forgotten.

A woman in the home is the same as an administrator in business. Administration is a gift from God. If you don't have it, ask Him for it. That is the description of the woman in Proverbs 31. Learn to administrate until you are good at it.

Most women take a shopping list to the store, but they also need daily lists. Keep store lists handy and available so others can add to them when supplies run low or the needs arise. Get everyone cooperating so it is not your burden alone.

Do not try to do everything by memory because your memory will fail, burn out or put itself on overload. The computer I am using, at times, will suddenly flash "memory full." Your mind is like that and will turn off at times. Write it down! Part of the "harried-housewife syndrome" is trying to remember everything and living with a cluttered mind, which eliminates peace from the soul.

Good administrators are invaluable in business, government and home. In the Godhead, the Lord Jesus Christ is the Visionary, the Holy Spirit is the Administrator, and the Father is the Governor for the Church. Daily, devotionally, ask for the Holy Spirit's gifts to be made manifest in your life. Let God maximize your abilities.

I realize mine is a man's point of view, but Nancy has more to say from the woman's perspective on this critical subject.

NANCY

While contemplating ministry in the home and motherhood, I happened to be on the telephone talking to my daughter, Lois. She and her husband, Rick, have given us two of the most beautiful, brilliant, loveable and enjoyable granddaughters the world has ever seen. And if you think I am prejudiced, you are right!

While I was talking to her, I asked her what being a mother meant to her. This was her reply: "Being a mother means never having a free moment, even on vacations. It means being responsible for little people twenty-four hours a day with never a day off."

I chimed in with the observation that even when our children are in their thirties, as Lois is, the responsibility is still there. We both laughed. She and I enjoy motherhood. I do not know of anyone who enjoys her children more or is a better mother without stress or strain than Lois. However, the fact of the matter is that we touched on a sober reality: Motherhood is a full-time job that never ends! Being a mother is a great and awesome responsibility. Many of us get married and can hardly wait for that first baby. All we can think of is that soft, warm, tiny mass of humanity.

What women usually do not think about are the sleepless nights, the mounds of dirty diapers, the feeding difficulties, the colic and all those other unpleasant things that rear their ugly heads during the course of infancy and the toddler stage.

"Will this ever end?" may be a mother's cry! The answer is obvious. Barring calamity, no, it will never end. But the joys of motherhood far outweigh the burden of responsibility.

Mothers imprint their attitudes and ideas onto the child's young, immature life. So it is very important what we are putting into that child. Are you implanting a fearful, critical attitude or a peaceful, loving, forgiving, God-fearing nature?

When my children were young, I guess I made every mistake a new mother can make. I am sure I was short-tempered at times. None of us is perfect. But, *it is what we do with our failures that counts.* Do we take them to the Lord and ask for forgiveness? Do we ask our children to forgive us when necessary?

Our attitudes toward the children and the constancy of living a godly life day by day are what will stay in their minds and hearts. That is what will give them a security in their identity to carry them through the crises and good times of later years. Providing you have worked on putting a God-consciousness into their spirits, they will have the marvelous assurance of who they are in God.

Also remember that each of your children has a different, unique personality. When Paul, as a young teenager, spent hours playing the guitar in his room, I had no idea he was composing songs that later blessed our congregation and others with their purity and simplicity.

Nor did I recognize Lois' propensity for debate (which sometimes we called "arguing") that presaged a successful career as a prosecuting attorney.

With Joann, I remember seeing her tie her shoes at a very early age, before kindergarten, and I was ashamed that I had not even tried to teach her that skill which she learned by herself. Then, in fifth grade, there was talk of skipping her to seventh grade. I realized she was smart, but what I did not realize was her extraordinary sensitivity to the world around her. Not until she was through school and going through a turbulent time spiritually did I develop an awareness that she, and the other children, were made up of spirit, soul and body, each uniquely different from the others.

My children still surprise me with some of the qualities they exhibit. I think, *Where did they ever learn that?* We have to remember we may not always see our children as they really are in God's eyes. We must discipline ourselves in prayer to learn what "makes them tick."

Edwin and I do not have a perfect family, but we have stayed on our knees, and God has been faithful. If you think you, or your children, cannot live up to God' greatest goals for your lives, quit trying to do it on your own. Let God be strong within you instead of trying to be strong for Him. We cannot impress God. But we are impressed by Him when we see what He makes of our lives. Release your children to God and allow them to achieve.

My daughters have struggled, as I did, with being working mothers. I have noticed, however, that every woman in Scripture worked or held some kind of title, although not always for pay. Every mother must examine her own heart about working outside the home, whether as a volunteer or for pay. What a fallacy to call a full-time homemaker a nonworking mother!

There are women who prefer outside involvement, even though they do not have to work. The Bible certainly teaches it is better to be busy than idle and that godly women adorn themselves with good works.[9] Idleness leads to gossip.[10] It also leads to fantasy and sexual immorality.[11] So the choice of whether or not to occupy yourself with work for pay is up to you, although the priorities of family first never changes.

If you find yourself in the workplace, earning a living for any reason, then by all means, get the best job possible, preferably one with a chance for advancement. If you have the talent and brains for a high-level job and the opportunity is there, then go for it! If you have to be away from your family anyway, at least make those hours worth your time and theirs.

There is a pitfall in career planning, however, which you will have to keep in balance—and that is the cost to your family.

Lois was in line for a promotion, but in observing the people already in that coveted post, she saw this would be a very time-consuming position that would require long hours both in the office and at home. She had had a taste of this occasionally, and it troubled her. Once, when she was engaged in some extra, very intensive work, she told me that even though she went home to be with her family, she was so preoccupied, she did not hear them when they attempted to converse with her. In one instance, her troubled little girl said, "Mom! I have asked you the same question five times, and you didn't hear me even once."

When the time came for the promotion, Lois very prayerfully and conscientiously turned it down. Since then, she and Rick have moved to an entirely new community where their workplaces are closer to home and their daughters' schools, and Lois is in an even more exciting position! God does lead and guide us, as He has promised in His Word.[12]

Whether or not you are working, every mother wonders, at times, if she is losing patience or sanity. A few years ago, I visited my son when his youngest child was barely three years old. My daughter-in-law, Judi, was being a lovely hostess and making sure I was comfortable.

The first morning she scurried around the kitchen, serving waffles to us all. When she handed me my plate, I looked down at a sight that would make a pre-schooler drool: buttered waffles covered with syrup and cut into bite-sized pieces. When Judi saw me hesitate, she looked at the plate and realized what she had done. We all laughed uproariously. Cutting everyone's food is the classic blooper of a mother of small children!

Judi found that being home continually with her children caused her mind to stagnate, so she looked for an outlet. She worked sporadically, choosing her own hours as a makeup artist, and finally started a business out of her own house. Now she is able to be with the children but have outside interests as well.

A mother with young children must be careful lest the cares of the world choke the life, or spirit, out of her.[13] When the pressure is on, it is easy to develop bad habits. One of those is to take out frustrations on the children. We must learn to accept our weaknesses as ours and not blame the children because we have let anxiety or pressure mount.

On the other hand, we cannot wait and let the father deal with the more serious issues. "Just wait until your father gets home!" is a phrase that, with a little bit of contemplation and calmness, could so often be avoided. A working father comes home from a turbulent world wanting a peaceful haven. He does not need his children dreading his return home, nor does he need a blow-by-blow account of every detail of the day.

The relationship with your children must never become a stumbling block to the relationship with your husband. Children need the benefits of a good marriage between their father and mother.

A common complaint among young mothers is the massive amount of work—cleaning up after more and more people in the house, mounds of laundry, hungry mouths to feed three times a day. Most young mothers lead strenuous lives. But if you plan carefully and train the children (and your husband!) to help, you can do it. I was surprised to read a doctor's report suggesting that by eight years of age, children should be responsible for cleaning their own bedrooms, and by ten, they should be able to do any major chore around the house, even vacuuming.

I discovered this for myself when my children were very small. Many a night, as we pioneered a new church with three children under four years of age, I crawled into bed on legs that felt hollowed out and barely functional. I will never forget the feeling! Then Edwin began ministering as a missionary-evangelist and was frequently away on trips that lasted days, weeks and sometimes months. To add to the difficulty of being alone with the children, I worked full time and drove an hour each way to work. Those were not easy years, but God gave me wisdom.

I realized that if I wanted the children to help me with chores when they were older, I might as well start right then. (Later I discovered this was scriptural!—Hebrews 12:11.) So on Saturday mornings, they each had an assignment. Even the youngest at five years old had a dust cloth and dusted the entire house herself. Granted, I had to go behind them and pick up what they missed after they were in bed at night, but after a few years of investing this way, I reaped big dividends. They all became valuable helps to me around the house.

There is only one regret that remains from those years, and that is when Paul showed an interest in cooking, I did not teach him. (Yes, I confess to stereotype thinking!) Not only did I live to regret stifling that creative outlet, but so does his wife, Judi!

Another thing God showed me during that time was how to spend time alone with Him regardless of how full my days were. The plan He gave me was both simple and effective once I implemented it. Here it is: I put the children to bed earlier!

I knew Paul had a flashlight under his covers and he was reading, and I could hear Lois and Joann giggling. Nevertheless, I was marvelously alone for a few quiet moments in the evenings to enjoy the Lord—just Him and me. That relationship is the most important to keep intact.

As Edwin says, "It is more important to talk to the Lord about your children than to your children about the Lord."

One more thing I want to add: Did you ever treat your child or children in a way you had vowed never to treat them? Perhaps your parents treated you that way, and long ago, you vowed you would never do the same thing. If this has happened to you, examine your heart for unforgiveness toward your parents. You may hardly be aware of the resentment that you still feel over those incidents that disturbed you. When you become aware of hidden resentments, you can be released by forgiving those who hurt you, whether or not they are still living, and asking the Lord to take it out of your life.

Overall, it is your attitude toward your child that will linger on. An attitude of appreciation toward children is what I suggest as the antidote for attitudes of resentment, jealousy or frustration. Choose to appreciate the great attributes God has placed within the life of each one.

Thank God every day for your husband and/or children. They are His gifts to you.[14] Thank Him for your home. Thank Him for the peace that He floods your heart with. Psalm 91, Isaiah 65:24, John 15:7, 1 Chronicles 16:11, Psalm 25:5 and Isaiah 30:15 are great scriptures to start the day with as you prepare to minister in the home.

CHAPTER TWELVE

THE MATURE WOMAN

EDWIN

I was in Niagara Falls, that great honeymooners' paradise, speaking at a conference for couples. One evening, I asked how many were on their honeymoon. One couple said they were celebrating their fortieth anniversary and honeymoon combined, and many people in the audience laughed.

Looking at the somewhat young audience, I told them they were laughing out of turn. "You don't quit making love when you grow older," I explained, "you just quit making babies!" When their laughter died down, I added, "And besides, it is better the older you get because you know what you are doing."

They roared with laughter and applause.

But it is true. We go through seasons of life as we grow older, and each season has a glory of its own. Whether that season is a blessing or a curse depends on the choices and attitudes of each individual. Your later years can either be your greatest years or your most lonely and miserable.

Why retire and vegetate when there is still so much living to do?

Widows and widowers need not be lonely or nonproductive. Many do not stop living when their spouse dies; they simply start a new life.

When her husband, David, died, our friend, Arline, suffered over his death. He had been sick for years and spent his last months deteriorating from Alzheimer's disease in a convalescent hospital. During those difficult days, she ministered to his every need. At his death, she cried with the family.

After his death, a metamorphosis began to take place in Arline. She realized that her life was not over, that she did not "die" with her husband and that God was not through with her yet. She moved, bought new clothes, adopted a new hairstyle and started going places she had never been and doing things she had never done during her forty-nine years of marriage. Today, she is enjoying the years she has left and is making every moment count.

Death is an abnormality. Man was never created to die but to live eternally with God. No matter how prepared for it you may be, death is always a shock.

Ministry to and for widows is given distinct direction in the Bible. Honoring widows is a scriptural injunction,[1] and ministering to their needs is a requirement of "pure religion."[2] Ministers and churches are increasingly providing for the needs of the "mature members" of the congregation, but of the need scripturally to provide for the care of widows, most seem to be ignorant.

I am equally amazed at how often churches have young associate pastor's wives teaching women how to take care of the family when Scripture explicitly gives that responsibility to the "aged women."[3]

Why waste wisdom, experience and knowledge? Do not ignore the aged women and let it be a loss to you, your family and your church! Do not think your religion is "pure" when you do not care for the widows!

And for the aged women: Whatever you do, do not die physically, spiritually or mentally—and let it be a loss to society! Pour all your knowledge and experience into young

men and women. Why make them reinvent the wheel?
Each generation is to be enriched by the previous, but
this will not happen if the older generation does not make
it happen or if they are prevented from doing so by the
ignorance of the younger generation's leaders.

Recently, I found out why these years are called "the
sunset years." Nancy and I were invited to spend some time at
the condominium of our friends Jim and Betty in Princeville,
Hawaii, where I was supposed to work on a book. Their place
sits almost at the end of a road to the beach.

A day of working in the morning and lolling on the
beach in the afternoon was followed by a shower and
dressing Hawaiian-style. Then we strolled to a place on a
cliff overlooking the ocean below.

Around us, slowly but surely, others gathered who
were as intent as we were on the evening's activity: We
watched the sunset.

Night after night, those of us on the island gathered
and spent time watching the sun go down. Each night the
view varied. Each sunset had a glory all its own. Something
awe-inspiring, majestic, hallowed, warm and romantic was
there. Our eyes could never behold all the glory. No photo-
graph could retain it. We had to return each evening to
drink our fill again.

Just so, there is a glory to every age of life and to old
age as well.[4] Each day, each month, each year for each person
holds an attraction and glory all its own—if we just take the
time and make the effort to behold and enjoy it. Each age is a
time and opportunity never experienced before.

At both our daughters' graduations from college, there
were gray-haired people in the class. Those senior classmates now
had time to go back to college and finish. Second careers are
common for retired soldiers. Many of them make more money
after retirement than they ever did in military service.

The reason many people die soon after retirement is
because they lose their goals. New goals give new energy.
When people stop setting productive goals and desire only the goal

of making themselves happy, we call it "the sin of being fifty." Happiness is never a goal but always a by-product. Happiness comes when we strive for a worthy goal. When people shift from productive, worthwhile goals to the unworthy goal of making themselves happy, they become negative instead of positive. With a negative attitude, they complain, criticize and air their prejudices instead of experiencing the true happiness they seek.

If you are in these "sunset years," do not let the sun go down ingloriously. Make the months and years productive, fulfilled, enjoyable and blessed. Just because age takes its toll, and your physical body becomes slowed or impaired, does not mean you must quit mentally or spiritually. Do not vegetate as a "couch potato," watching television and living vicariously through someone else's imagination and fantasy.

It is still a real world.

There is still real living to do.

These can be your greatest years.

Nancy can help you know what to do.

NANCY

You may be young or old, but I would like to shed a little light on some scriptures and how they pertain to you—particularly in your latter years.

Second Peter 1:2-10 reads almost like a list of things to watch for as we mature:

> Grace and peace be multiplied unto you through the knowledge of God and of Jesus our Lord.
>
> According as his divine power hath given unto us all things that pertain unto life and godliness, through the knowledge of him that hath called us to glory and virtue:
>
> Whereby are given unto us exceeding great and precious promises: that by these ye might be partakers of the divine nature, having escaped the corruption that is in the world through lust,

And beside this, giving all diligence, add
to your faith virtue; and to virtue knowledge;

And to knowledge temperance;
and to temperance patience; and to
patience godliness;

And to godliness brotherly kindness;
and to brotherly kindness charity.

For if these things be in you, and
abound, they make you that ye shall
neither be barren nor unfruitful in the
knowledge of our Lord Jesus Christ.

But he that lacketh these things is blind,
and cannot see afar off, and hath forgotten
that he was purged from his old sins.

Wherefore the rather, brethren, give diligence to make your calling and election sure:
for if ye do these things, ye shall never fall.

The epistle of Paul to Titus specifically addresses the
mature woman:

The aged women likewise, that they
be in behaviour as becometh holiness, not
false accusers, not given to much wine,
teachers of good things;

That they may teach the younger
women to be sober, to love their husbands,
to love their children,

To be discreet, chaste, keepers at home,
good, obedient to their own husbands, that
the word of God be not blasphemed.

Titus 2:3-5

Perhaps you are a young woman and have wondered
why some older people are lonely, introverted or self-
centered and why others are such a joy to be around.
Perhaps you have looked at them and wondered what you
will be like at that age.

For a moment, consider the physiological aspect of growing
older. The dividing line seems to be at the cessation of menstrual

periods. Many women experience things such as "hot flashes." There may be insomnia, anxiety, depression, an increase or decrease in the sex drive. The body is in transition. It is losing the ability to create estrogen. This is called menopause.

Medically speaking, one has not gone through menopause until there is a complete cessation of the menstrual periods for twelve months. Menopause can occur in women as early as late thirties and as late as mid-fifties. Many doctors prescribe an estrogen supplement for women in menopause; however, there is a wide difference of opinion on the medical treatment of these symptoms. Pray about how you personally treat the signs of inevitable aging.

If you are in this season of life, I have good news for you! Just as you thought at one time there would never be life after thirty or forty, yet you discovered there was, you will be surprised at your swift recovery and return to stability after menopause. Many women find themselves more energetic, readier to try something new, and sexual activity no longer brings the subtle fear of pregnancy.

The "change of life" is not the end of life—it is just the beginning of another stage!

These days, with the advances in medicine, nutrition, laborsaving devices and our general superior knowledge to that of our forefathers, women can expect to live twenty-five years after menopause. So we have plenty of opportunities to do many things that we were not able to do before.

For one thing, we have come to an age when life should be much more peaceful. By now, we should have resolved most of our intolerances and conflicts with our spouses. As I said earlier, the breakup of many marriages after twenty-five or thirty years is because of growing intolerance with one's mate. We must constantly work on our relationships with our husbands, praying and then believing God to accomplish the work, and allowing Him to make us more patient, understanding and tolerant year by year.

Actually, it is surprising how many minor annoyances can become major sources of unhappiness. Edwin once counseled a couple who had many differences that were great enough to drive them apart but which were actually minor. The husband, during the course of counseling, brought up the fact that his wife always put the toilet tissue on the holder one way and he liked it another. Now you may laugh over that, but it happened. The way the toilet tissue was mounted was a source of friction in the marriage! Common courtesy was evidently not prevalent in their lives.

As we grow older, we must learn to allow each other freedom to be ourselves. If we can do this, we can reach a very high level of contentment in our lives. We will let go of the minor annoyances that drove us apart in earlier years.

Children, for the most part, are on their own by this time, hopefully doing well with the great training they have received from their parents. If not, and you are a newly-born Christian, remember God's promise that not only will you be saved, but your household as well, and pray accordingly.[5]

In this season of life, the problems with your children generally are those you create by not accepting their spouses. This attitude leads to all kinds of trouble during family holidays and special occasions. Need I say more? Keep the calm and forgiving attitude you have developed even when dealing with in-laws. It makes for a much more peaceful life for everyone.

When the mid-years come, if we have been industrious and worked on our relationships with others, there comes a certain stability of life that we have not known before. Many of the conflicts that affect the teen years, the years of early marriage or single living, of striving on our jobs, of pursuing dreams (some valid, others not), of ego trips, of striving to "be somebody," the vanity and envy and lust for power that may have been there in the past—all these things dissipated for the most part as we discovered the more important things in life.

The bitterness over lost opportunities, the regrets, the thoughts of "who did us wrong" can be resolved in prayer before an almighty and forgiving God and the principle of "release" we have previously mentioned several times.

Now—let's say all these conflicts are resolved. There you are with no animosity in your marriage, good relationships with your children and toward everyone around you; you are forgiving, accepting, loving and full of the goodness of God. Then whole new vistas of opportunity open before you!

The age group from forty-five to sixty-four has the greatest buying power in America today. Advertisers are increasingly concentrating on them. Retailers are discovering that grandpa is not sitting on his porch whittling, and grandma is not a slave to her kitchen anymore.

"Senior citizens" today are doing all sorts of traveling, learning, teaching, civic activities and more. They are involved in life! The late Maria von Trapp, whose life was the basis for the movie, *The Sound of Music*, learned to ski and ride a horse when she was around sixty. Former President Ronald Reagan led the United States until three weeks before his seventy-eighth birthday. His first week out of office, he began working on his memoirs, set a full calendar for lecturing and began choosing what cause he would champion to help others. Mrs. Reagan was quoted as saying, "We do not believe in retirement."

Look at many aged United States Supreme Court justices and government workers in high echelons of other countries—they have very active minds! Their reasoning ability is excellent, and their wisdom from years of experience is invaluable. Why do some people think older people have lost their reasoning ability? I believe it is because many older people let their minds lapse into disuse!

That brings us back to the scriptures from 2 Peter, chapter 1, that I quoted earlier in this chapter. In verses 8 and 15, Peter says to grow in faith with all diligence in order not to be barren or unfruitful. The thought is of investing. Just as you invest money for your retirement, you must invest spiritually as well.

My daughter, Joann, went to a financial seminar recently, and the things the instructor said made a great impact on her. For one, he had them visualize how much money passes through one's hands in a lifetime. Yet how many people end up in rest homes or barely squeaking by on Social Security or pension checks? Joann began to think of when she worked in such a rest home and how many people, the majority there, ended up friendless. Yet surely, they had many friends through the years. Worse than being alone, they had become lonely.

What are we investing in? Are we going to end up friendless? In poverty? Do our children avoid calling us because of our complaints? You must add to your faith virtue, knowledge, temperance and patience. If you are a widow, or intimately know someone who is widowed, you know how difficult it is to adjust to being alone. If your relationship with Jesus Christ was built "with all diligence" throughout your married life, then the adjustment is much easier because you know God as your Father, Husband, Comforter and Friend.[6]

To your faith, add brotherly kindness and charity, which is love. In the last pastorate Edwin and I had, there was a little grandmother who was a member of our congregation. She was a delight! She lived alone but was never lonely. Everyone loved her. She was about ninety years old, but she did not act like it. Instead of wearing conservative pumps, she sometimes wore bright red shoes—rakishly red, with good-sized bows!

She was always concerned about others. Once when she was hospitalized before her death, some of the young people visited her. In reporting on their visit, they marveled that she had said nothing about her illness. Instead, she was concerned about those young people, asking them about themselves and encouraging them. She displayed such a bright, cheery manner that they came from the visit edified and built up in their faith.

What are you investing? Titus 2:3, 4 speaks very plainly about aged women of proven reputation and character teaching the younger women. I think of another pastorate we had in Northern California. We had a blessing there in an older lady who taught many of us the fine art of entertaining crowds. She taught us how to set a beautiful table and how to make fancy tea sandwiches and hors d'oeuvres for weddings and parties.

We discovered this was something she had done in previous churches as well. I never heard a cross word or sharp comment pass though her lips, although there was plenty of opportunity as she orchestrated crowds of women to prepare receptions and parties just right! She was an inspiration to all the ladies there right down to the teenagers. You see, she was investing her time and talent into the younger women of the congregation. By doing so, she stayed young and fresh herself.

Teaching the younger women does not necessarily mean leading a Bible study or standing in front of a group. Did you teach your children by lecture or by example? Perhaps you are not comfortable with lecturing someone, but you can help a young wife get her house in order. You could get a new baby on a schedule for a young mother or show her how to stop her toddler from sucking his thumb. You can teach the woman who works how to clean house more efficiently, so she can put in those hours with the Lord that she cannot quite find time for now.

You can show someone how to use a concordance and how to memorize Scripture. You can teach what many young people no longer learn to do—freeze foods, can, make jellies, quilt, knit and sew. You can teach them the difference between weeds and new grass or perhaps how to cut hair.

One of Edwin's aunts in her nineties stays active even though her frail body can no longer move as easily as it used to. Her activity is to influence people politically to vote for her choice of candidate. She monitors the television, stays abreast of every interview, debate and announcement and relays the information to anyone who will listen. Those who are caught up in the busyness of life could appreciate her information and sage advice.

In our displaced society, many young couples live far from either set of parents. There are actually advertisements in many newspapers today by women who desire a "grandmother" in their home. Civic groups are matching grandmothers to children in various programs.

I think of the many women in their mature years who have not made this kind of investment in young people's lives. Yet they do not know why they are depressed and unhappy. Their friends of the same age start to die off, and over the course of the years, their telephones stop ringing. They outlive their friends and their husbands and are soon left alone, lonely and depressed.

If this is your lot or you see that it is the plight of older women in your church, talk to the pastor about teaching the younger women. You will be surprised at how much wisdom and experience is just sitting there in the pew. The time invested will be reciprocated, also, when the older women gain a new outlook. They become more optimistic and are surrounded by burgeoning life instead of death. This is why God's pattern makes so much sense.

If you are a mature woman, drop some of those old expressions that no one today understands. Update yourself! It is so much easier to do this if you are around younger people. Keep your lifelong friends, by all means, but invest some of your time in cultivating new friendships with younger people. You have the experience, the wisdom, the knowledge of God because you have proved Him time and time again. This is the giving of yourself which is really what Peter meant when he said you will not be barren or unfruitful in the knowledge of Jesus.

If we truly know Jesus, we know He came to serve. He took a towel and washed the disciples' feet. He took the way of the cross for your sins and mine. He traveled the dusty roads to heal the sick, bind up the bruised, heal the broken-hearted. This is the knowledge of Jesus that He wants us to have and pass on to others in order to be diligent and productive *all* of our lives, not just when we are young and in perfect health.[7]

My daughter knows an elderly lady who took in a disadvantaged girl for a short period of time. At first she was fearful, having never done this before. But what a blessing it proved to be! She was able to minister to the girl and, in turn, was blessed beyond description. She speaks of it so often, it appears to be one of the highlights of her old age.

Another friend of ours spent months before his death, even though incapacitated, taking in prayer requests and praying day and night for the needs of others.

Whatever we find in our hand to do, we are to do it with all our might![8] This is not a scripture for the young. It is applicable to all our lives, young and old. Every scripture in the Bible is for you. You never outgrow it. Never overuse it; never get to where you do not need it. Apply the Word in every situation, regardless of what age you live to! If you do, you will NEVER fall.[9]

ENDNOTES

INTRODUCTION

1 The Stephanie Brush column. Copyright ©1988.
   The Washington Post Writers' Group.
   Reprinted with permission.

CHAPTER 1

1 Bureau of Justice special report entitled
   "Preventing Domestic Violence Against Women,"
   August 1986, National Crime Survey.

2 Bureau of Justice Statistics, "Women, Violence and the
   Law," 1986 a fact sheet, U.S. House of Representatives
   Select Committee on Children, Youth and Families.

3 Genesis 1:26-28

4 John 4:32

5 Genesis 2:18

6 Genesis 2:7

7 Genesis 5:2

8 See 2 Chronicles 16:9

9 Luke 4:18

10 "Stand Amazed in the Presence of Jesus" by Charles
    H. Gabriel. From *Hymns of Glorious Praise,*
    Copyright © 1969, Gospel Publishing House,
    Springfield, Missouri.

11 Psalm 139:15, 16 TLB

12 Psalm 139:17, 18 TLB

13 Deuteronomy 7:9

14 Hebrews 13:5b, 8

CHAPTER 2

1 Exodus 3:8

2 1 Corinthians 10:6-10

3 Springdale, PA: Whitaker House, 1982.

4 1 Kings 19:5-9; Exodus 6:9

5 1 John 2:16

6 See Exodus 38:8; Deuteronomy 23:17; 1 Samuel 2:22

7 1 John 3:6

8 Numbers 11:6

9 James 5:16

10 Psalm 33:1

11 Matthew 17:5

12 Hebrews 5:7

13 *Webster's New World Dictionary,*
    2d college ed., s.v. "identity."

14 Hebrews 13:8

15 2 Timothy 2:22

16 Matthew 10:39

17 2 Timothy 2:13

18 Galatians 3:28

19 Ephesians 4:5

20 Colossians 1:27

21 See 1 Corinthians 10:11

22 1 Samuel 25:14-35

23 Hebrews 7:25;

Romans 8:34

CHAPTER 3

1 1 Samuel 25:3

2 1 Samuel 25:16

3 1 Samuel 25:28-32

4 1 Samuel 25:37, 38

5 Ruth 1-4

6 Colossians 4:5

7 Colossians 4:5 NIV

8 1 Kings 19:12

9 Psalm 18:35

10 "Sex Difference in Reasoning Skills Is on the Decline,

Research Finds," by Thomas H. Maugh II.

Copyright © 1989, *The Los Angeles Times.*

Home Edition, January 16, 1989,

Part I, p. 3. Reprinted by permission.

11 Deuteronomy 31:6

12 John 16:33

13 Joel 2:28, 29

14 Isaiah 32:9

15 2 Timothy 3:6 NIV

16   See Romans 6:16

17   Judges 5:7

18   Esther 1-10

19   Exodus 1:16, 17, 20, 21

20   Psalm 145:19

21   Isaiah 33:6

22   James 1:5 NIV

23   Jim Wright, *The Dallas Morning News*, April 14, 1987.

24   Galatians 5:1, 13

25   Proverbs 18:19

26   1 Kings 16:29-34; Revelation 2:18-26

27   1 Timothy 2:12

CHAPTER 4

1   Genesis 11:1-9

2   Acts 1:4

3   Acts 1:13; 2:1

4   Acts 2:4-6

5   See Genesis 1:26, 27

6   See Genesis 3:16

7   Galatians 3:13

8   1 Corinthians 11:3

9   1 Peter 3:7 TLB

10   Psalm 66:18

11   Hebrews 4:12

12   James 1:5

13   1 Peter 2:13; Ephesians 5:21

14   Philippians 2:4 AMP

15   Hebrews 12:9; James 4:6, 7

16   1 Samuel 8:7; 12:12

17   See James 3:7

18   John 13:3-5

19   Colossians 3:23, 24

20   1 John 3:22

21   Genesis 31:1-16

22   Luke 22:44 NIV

23   Hebrews 11

24   1 Peter 3:6

25   Matthew 22:21

26   Romans 8:28

27   See Hebrews 5:7

28   Matthew 21:12

29   1 Peter 3:1

30   Matthew 23:3

31   Matthew 23:27

32   Deuteronomy 29:18

CHAPTER 5

1   Psalm 50:21; Isaiah 47:3; 51:12; Hosea 11:9

2   Genesis 16:13

3 Deuteronomy 31:6, 8; Joshua 1:5

4 Exodus 3:2; 13:21; Ezekiel 1:27, 28; Daniel 7:9;
   Matthew 17:2

5 Psalm 50:21; Isaiah 40:18, 25; 46:5, 9; 47:3;
   Numbers 23:19; Deuteronomy 4:15, 16; Job 9:32;
   Hosea 11:9

6 Ephesians 3:20

7 1 John 4:8

8 Philippians 3:13

9 Micah 7:19

10 John 20:22, 23

11 Matthew 6:15; Psalm 66:18

12 Matthew 18:35; Mark 11:25, 26

13 Luke 11:4

14 Malachi 4:6

CHAPTER 6

1 1 Kings 18:17, 18

2 Ephesians 5:23-32

3 Genesis 17:10

4 Colossians 2:11, 12; 1 Peter 3:21; 1 Corinthians 11:25

5 Hebrews 13:4

6 1 Timothy 4:4

7 Genesis 2:15

8 Hosea 4:6

9 "Teen Sex Survey in the Evangelical Church," Copyright © 1987, Josh McDowell Ministry.

10 Ecclesiastes 8:11

11 Romans 2:21-24

12 *Communication, Sex and Money*

13 *Sexual Integrity: A Sexual Revolution Called Purity*

14 Proverbs 18:19

CHAPTER 7

1 John 16:21

2 Ecclesiastes 7:3

3 Proverbs 22:1

4 Tim Appelo, "Welcome to the '90s," *Savvy Woman*, January 1989, pp. 77-82, 110.

5 Hebrews 13:8

6 John 16:13

7 Philippians 4:7

8 Joel 2:29 NIV

9 1 Corinthians 7:34

10 Matthew 6:33

11 Genesis 12:11-16; 20:2

12 Genesis 24

CHAPTER 8

1 Genesis 2:24

2 Ephesians 5:25

3 1 Timothy 2:5

4 Colossians 1:20

5 1 Kings 16-21

6 1 Kings 19:1, 2

7 Genesis 3:6

8 Genesis 39:7-20

9 Isaiah 33:1

10 Revelation 2:20

11 Revelation 2:21-23

12 Proverbs 12:4 TLB

13 Isaiah 58:8

14 Romans 15:5

CHAPTER 9

1 Proverbs 21:9

2 Romans 10:17

3 Romans 12:10

4 Luke 10:5

5 Titus 2:4, 5

6 Psalm 66:18

7 1 Peter 5:8

8   1 John 2:1

9   James 5:16; Hebrews 11:6

CHAPTER 10

1   Genesis 3:6

2   John 10:10

3   Hebrews 2:14; 1 John 3:8

4   John 8:44; 14:6

5   2 Corinthians 6:14

6   Proverbs 4:7

7   Proverbs 3:16, 17 TLB

8   James 3:15

9   Proverbs 3:7

10   Proverbs 9:10

11   Hebrews 2:14; 1 John 3:8

12   1 Corinthians 1:30

13   James 1:5

14   John 8:44

15   1 Peter 5:8

16   Daniel 6:22

17   1 Peter 3:1-5 KJV, AMP

18   2 Corinthians 3:18

19   Proverbs 15:1

20   Proverbs 8:1

21 Amos 4:13

22 Psalm 16:11

23 Matthew 19:6

24 1 John 1:6-9

25 Ephesians 4:32

26 1 Corinthians 6:19

27 Matthew 7:2-4

28 Matthew 11:30

29 Philippians 2:12

CHAPTER 11

1 Proverbs 17:15 TLB

2 Ephesians 6:12

3 2 Timothy 2:13

4 3 John 4

5 Proverbs 31:28

6 Jeremiah 30:11

7 Ephesians 5:16; Colossians 4:5

8 Proverbs 19:3

9 1 Timothy 2:9, 10; Philippians 2:14-16

10 1 Timothy 5:13

11 Ezekiel 16:49; Jude 7

12 Isaiah 58:11; John 16:13

13 Mark 4:19

14 Psalm 127:3

CHAPTER 12

1 1 Timothy 5:3

2 James 1:27

3 Titus 2:3-5

4 Proverbs 20:29

5 Acts 16:31

6 Psalm 68:5; Isaiah 51:12; Deuteronomy 10:17, 18;
   Proverbs 15:25 AMP

7 Titus 3:14

8 Colossians 3:23

9 2 Peter 1:10

The illustrations in this book were based on the lives of real people. Their identities, however, were completely concealed by fictitious names, occupations and/or geographical regions. The only exceptions are the Coles' lifelong friends, Ralph and Esther Calkins, and public figures. Any other similarities to actual people are unintentional.

MANHOOD GROWTH PLAN

Order the corresponding workbook for each book, and study the first four Majoring In Men® Curriculum books in this order:

MAXIMIZED MANHOOD: Realize your need for God in every area of your life and start mending relationships with Christ and your family.

COURAGE: Make peace with your past, learn the power of forgiveness and the value of character. Let yourself be challenged to speak up for Christ to other men.

COMMUNICATION, SEX AND MONEY: Increase your ability to communicate, place the right values on sex and money in relationships, and greatly improve relationships, whether married or single.

STRONG MEN IN TOUGH TIMES: Reframe trials, battles and discouragement in light of Scripture and gain solid footing for business, career, and relational choices in the future.

Choose five of the following books to study next. When you have completed nine books, if you are not in men's group, you can find a Majoring In Men® group near you and become "commissioned" to minister to other men.

DARING: Overcome fear to live a life of daring ambition for Godly pursuits.

MAJORING IN MEN® CURRICULUM

SEXUAL INTEGRITY: Recognize the sacredness of the sexual union, overcome mistakes and blunders and commit to righteousness in your sexuality.

UNIQUE WOMAN: Discover what makes a woman tick, from adolescence through maturity, to be able to minister to a spouse's uniqueness at any age.

NEVER QUIT: Take the ten steps for entering or leaving any situation, job, relationship or crisis in life.

REAL MAN: Discover the deepest meaning of Christlikeness and learn to exercise good character in times of stress, success or failure.

POWER OF POTENTIAL: Start making solid business and career choices based on Biblical principles while building core character that affects your entire life.

ABSOLUTE ANSWERS: Adopt practical habits and pursue Biblical solutions to overcome "prodigal problems" and secret sins that hinder both success and satisfaction with life.

TREASURE: Practice Biblical solutions and principles on the job to find treasures such as the satisfaction of exercising integrity and a job well done.

IRRESISTIBLE HUSBAND: Avoid common mistakes that sabotage a relationship and learn simple solutions and good habits to build a marriage that will consistently increase in intensity for decades.

MAJORING IN MEN® CURRICULUM

CHURCH GROWTH PLAN
STRONG - SUSTAINABLE - SYNERGISTIC

THREE PRACTICAL PHASES TO A POWERFUL MEN'S MOVEMENT IN YOUR CHURCH

Phase One:
- Pastor disciples key men/men's director using Maximized

Manhood system.
- Launch creates momentum among men
- Church becomes more attractive to hold men who visit
- Families grow stronger
- Men increase bond to pastor

Phase Two:
- Men/men's director teach other men within the church
- Increased tithing and giving by men
- Decreased number of families in crisis
- Increased mentoring of teens and children
- Increase of male volunteers
- Faster assimilation for men visitors - clear path for pastor to connect with new men
- Men pray regularly for pastor

Phase Three:
- Men teach other men outside the church and bring them to Christ
- Increased male population and attraction to a visiting man, seeing a place he belongs
- Stronger, better-attended community outreaches
- Men are loyal to and support pastor

This system enables the pastor to successfully train key leaders, create momentum, build a church that attracts and holds men who visit, and disciple strong men.

CONTACT
MAJORING IN MEN® CURRICULUM
817-437-4888
admin@ChristianMensNetwork.com

Christian Men's Network
P.O. Box 3
Grapevine, TX 76099

Great discounts available.

Start your discipleship TODAY!

Call today for group discounts
and coaching opportunities.

FREE DVD!
Send your name and address to:
office@ChristianMensNetwork.com
We'll send you a FREE full-length DVD
with ministry for men.
(Limit one per person.)

ABOUT THE AUTHORS

Edwin Louis Cole, together with his wife Nancy Corbett Cole and their family, built a global organization called Christian Men's Network that "majored in men" in ministry.

Edwin Louis Cole mentored hundreds of thousands of people through challenging events and powerful books that have become the most widely-used Christian men's resources in the world. He is known for pithy statements and a confrontational style that demanded social responsibility and family leadership.

After serving as a pastor, evangelist, and Christian television pioneer, and at an age when most men were retiring, he followed his greatest passion—to lead men into Christlikeness, which he called "real manhood."

Ed Cole was a real man through and through. A loving son to earthly parents and the heavenly Father. Devoted husband to the "loveliest lady in the land," Nancy Corbett Cole. Dedicated father to three and, over the years, accepting the role of "father" to thousands. A reader, a thinker, a visionary. A man who made mistakes, learned lessons, then shared the wealth of his wisdom with men around the world. The Christian Men's Network he founded in 1977 is still a vibrant, global ministry. Unquestionably, he was the greatest men's minister of his generation.

facebook.com/EdwinLouisCole